Kissing Toads

The Ultimate Online dating toolbox for women over 50

Julie Greig

First published by Ultimate World Publishing 2023
Copyright © 2023 Julie Greig

ISBN

Paperback: 978-1-922982-74-2
Ebook: 978-1-922982-75-9

Julie Greig has asserted her rights under the Copyright, Designs and Patents Act 1988 to be identified as the author of this work. The information in this book is based on the author's experiences and opinions. The publisher specifically disclaims responsibility for any adverse consequences which may result from use of the information contained herein. Permission to use information has been sought by the author. Any breaches will be rectified in further editions of the book.

All rights reserved. No part of this publication may be reproduced, stored in or introduced into a retrieval system, or transmitted in any form, or by any means (electronic, mechanical, photocopying, recording or otherwise) without the prior written permission of the author. Any person who does any unauthorised act in relation to this publication may be liable to criminal prosecution and civil claims for damages. Enquiries should be made through the publisher.

Cover design: Ultimate World Publishing
Layout and typesetting: Ultimate World Publishing
Editor: Vanessa McKay

Ultimate World Publishing
Diamond Creek,
Victoria Australia 3089
www.writeabook.com.au

Reading Julie's book was like having a chat about dating over a coffee with a friend. Her book shares many experiences I can relate to. I laughed and cried, and I was thinking, this is me; I've met those toads, and I know how they can drag you down.

Online dating is not an easy topic to talk about, particularly when you are over 50 and everyone thinks you should have your life together. Kissing Toads is encouraging. It makes it clear that it's okay to talk about online dating. It's okay to accept not all relationships will work out how you want them to, and it's okay to make your own rules.

Julie's book, her shared experiences, her toolbox, and checklists are a great 'go to' while you are navigating your way through dating online.

Kissing Toads was easy to read and a true insight into the electronic dating world from someone who has been there and done that. The book's focus on safety, wellbeing and positive self-awareness makes it a must read.

For any woman getting back into the world of dating, Kissing Toads is a highly recommended read.

Michelle Gray

It takes a brave soul to put themselves back out there in today's dating world, especially after loss.

Reading this book was an emotional ride. I got teary, I giggled, and I realised my sister is still the strongest woman I know!

Here's to family, girlfriends, extended family, sisters, wine o'clock and being smart enough to recognise toads.

Sue Oakford

Kissing Toads is a beautifully written book that explores the ups and downs of navigating the world of online dating as Julie finds herself back in the dating game after many years. Despite the early setback with a string of toads, Julie never loses hope and continues to search for the perfect match. And then she met the Frog - and we are treated to a happily ever after ending. But more than just a guidebook, Kissing Toads embarks on a journey of self-discovery, a lesson in self-care and self-worth. This book delivers a powerful message for all readers, whether single or in a relationship. Overall, Kissing Toads is a good read that will make you smile, cry and will leave you feeling inspired.

Zetty MY, MMC

A truly inspiring and practical read. Presented as a toolkit for women over 50, covering a multitude of concerns. This book is relevant to women of all ages and a great memory jogger. Too many books are either derived from dry research or vague commonsense without any practical foundation. The author has navigated the online dating minefield and draws on lived experiences. What she has done, we can do too. This book is a practical guide as to how. Tip: speed read it before a date and step out in confidence.

Sharon Ruddleston Int'l MMktg, MBA, CPM, FIML
Founder of *'Women Who Roar'*

Dedication

To all the women who want another chance at sharing the 'how was your day?' A glass of wine and a walk along the beach with a special someone.

Disclaimer

This book represents the author's recollection of experiences throughout her somewhat bumpy journey using online dating. To protect the privacy of certain individuals you will meet in the book names and identifying details have been changed.

Neither the author nor publisher is engaged in professional dating advice or services to the reader. The ideas, suggestions, and procedures provided in this book are not intended as a substitute for seeking professional guidance.

Neither the author or publisher shall be held liable nor responsible for any loss or damage allegedly arising from any suggestion or information contained in this book.

Should the reader have concerns for their safety or feel their wellbeing is compromised, please seek the appropriate help:

For Australian readers -
Police emergency – 000
Lifeline Australia – 131 144
1800Respect -1800 737 732

Contents

Dedication	v
Disclaimer	vii
How to use this book	xi
Introduction	1
Chapter 1: Does this dating thing come with a rulebook?	5
Chapter 2: What's the plan?	7
Chapter 3: Tom, Dick or Harry?	11
Chapter 4: Dating sites... What to say, what to do	15
Chapter 5: And so it begins	21
Chapter 6: Back to the drawing board	27
Chapter 7: It's all about love and being loved	29
Chapter 8: The finding love journey	33
Chapter 9: Finding another fish in the ocean	37
Chapter 10: Getting off the dating roller coaster	41
Chapter 11: Meet the toads	45
Chapter 12: Beware of the wolf (Aka –hero toads)	55
Chapter 13: Meet Stu	61
Chapter 14: How to watch for Red Flags	69

Kissing Toads

Chapter 15: And now for the other toad	71
Chapter 16: Meet Pete	75
Chapter 17: One of life's greatest treasures	81
Chapter 18: The lonely hearts club	89
Chapter 19: Meet Tom	93
Chapter 20: It's not a crying shame	103
Chapter 21: Times are a changing, are you?	105
Chapter 22: Let's talk about sex	109
Chapter 23: It's definitely not just me	119
Chapter 24: Down right dirty!	123
Chapter 25: Meet Terry	129
Chapter 26: Meet James	135
Chapter 27: Me time, you time, we all need our time	141
Chapter 28: Yes! There is a happy ever after	145
The toad refresher! (And where to learn more)	157
Important things to remember	159
Modern dating etiquette	161
The first date	163
Red flag alerts –and this is just some of them	165
The tool box items	169
The tick box checklist	171
The dating dictionary	173
Reference links for information you might want to read	177
About the Author	179
Acknowledgements	181
Things for me to note	185

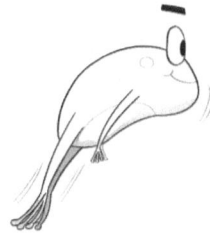
How to use this book

Start with a cup of courage, a clear mindset, a big spoon of self-worth and sprinkle with belief, then:

Grab a coffee or pour a wine and make yourself comfortable.

Read this book from cover to cover. It won't take long.

Remember this book is a guide, a navigational tool for your journey; refer to it as often as you want.

Never lose sight of what's important to you.

Take note of the rules, adopt mine, or make some of your own.

Learn how to recognise the toads; you are bound to meet some.

Remind yourself that you won't always get things right and that's okay.

Keep in mind that you learn from experience, the good, and the bad.

Kissing Toads

Take note about staying safe and being aware.

Rejection is hard, but shit happens.

Don't expect to find your perfect match overnight – good things take time.

Remember, everyone's journey is different, and your journey is unique. It's about you.

Get out there, check out the dating sites, test the water, and have fun!

Introduction

'How many toads do you kiss until you find a frog? You know; the one that turns into a handsome prince, the one who ticks all the boxes'

Meet me! Children all grown up, grandchildren, wonderful marriage, and then something went horribly wrong. What was once my perfect world had just been hit for a sixer. Life was to change forever. Here I was, 54 and suddenly a widow, adjusting to whatever life threw at me, alone.

Life can be cruel and it can leave you empty and alone and after a few years of talking to the cat and staring at the wall, you soon tell yourself it's time to put the big girl pants on and start making a new life, create a whole new world just for me or as I call it - time for a Plan B!

Time to decide; do I want to stay here on my own and turn into an old lady whose only friends are a million cats? Or do I want to get out there and enjoy what life I have while I can?

I eventually opt for Plan B - simple coffee dates with girlfriends, sometimes a dinner at the local hotel. Going to a movie alone or with

Kissing Toads

friends, it doesn't matter. It doesn't matter what you do as long as you do it. As long as you put one foot in front of the other and step out that front door while you are telling yourself *you can do this*.

Tip: Those first few steps are a big deal, so treat yourself; a new dress or shoes or even a visit to the hairdresser. This is a big step you are taking, and something special helps you feel good.

That's it! Life can go on and it's okay to have a Plan B. It's nice to know that when you are ready, you can have some sort of normal life and it's okay to tell yourself it is time to move on and enjoy life. Things will never be what they were, and a huge part of your heart will always belong to someone very special, but a human heart is big and it has space in it for new passions, new desires, and even new people.

After a few years of life on my own, I wanted someone in my life again. I wanted to be back in a loving relationship. I wanted all of those experiences and feelings that go with growing old together. I didn't want to feel lonely anymore; then crash, bang, WTF – it gets scary. The feelings of guilt, betrayal and how on earth could I want to meet someone else? What was I thinking?

What would the kids think? What would friends and family think? It sounded too hard. Have I waited long enough? How long is long enough?

Pour me a coffee! No. Pour me a wine! This is all too much. So now sitting here I am telling the me of five years ago to **STOP**. Stop worrying about what everyone else might think. Stop feeling guilty, stop feeling like you are cheating. I have a right to be happy again. I have a right to laugh, to live life and maybe, even maybe, fall in love again and start a new journey.

Introduction

Kissing Toads

"It's okay to be scared. But you have to get out there, open up, love, make mistakes, learn, be stronger.
And start all over again."
(Anonymous)

Chapter 1

Does this dating thing come with a rulebook?

Everyone deserves to be happy, and happiness doesn't just happen. You have to make it happen. You have to find it, recognise it, and make it work. Happiness can come from companionship, from embracing life and being willing to take risks and see if there is someone out there who ticks all the boxes.

It's important to remember that those who really love you will be happy to see you happy again.

There are no written rules in the quest to find love again, but sometimes I think you need a few rules. Maybe not rules but protocols or something you can set your moral compass from.

Kissing Toads

Call them rules or call them protocols. It doesn't matter; it's all a measure of your values and self-worth. After all, I didn't ask for this and neither did a lot of other women out there.

So what are my rules?

Rule 1: You make the rules.

This rule is really important. You are you. No-one else can tell you what's good for you or what's right or wrong for you. **You make the rules.**

Rule 2: You have a right to change the rules.

Rule 3: If rule 1 fails, go back to rule 2.

These rules, my friends, I will refer to as the golden rules!

Chapter 2

What's the plan?

Once you have established your rules, then comes the next step; deciding what you want to do. This may be a short-term, a long-term or maybe even a five-year plan that is common in career planning. *Check with rule #1 if you aren't sure.*

This step can be a little challenging, no who am I kidding? It's totally overwhelming! This is where good friends come in (friends like mine!). Friends, good friends are great sounding boards and they can be good for reminding you of your own rules.

My friends are my extended family. Along with my boys, they are fun, loving, great drinking partners and they have always been there for my many ups and downs. They are definitely not for sale or loan.

Kissing Toads

For me, the first small steps back into the normal world were these outings with friends. Little step by little step, coffee outings turned into dinner outings, then dinner outings turned into pub quiz nights. Then came the dinner dances. Dinner, wine and dancing, yes dancing!

It's here some sort of normal starts to come back. The laughter and the fun returns and before long you are up dancing with new people (men) on the dance floor!

First it feels strange, after all you haven't danced with strangers for many years and you are no longer that 16-year-old girl who got her boogie shoes and blue jeans on every Friday night ready to dance the night away!

Panic sets in. What are the rules? Then I remind myself of rule #1, and this man, well, it's only a dance, and he is way too old for me. Then I discover he is younger than me and just looks old. Ouch! Is this older generation dating in the 21st century?

Is this how you meet people? God, I wish there was a simple instruction book on dating for the over fifty.

One thing you notice when you are bopping around on the dance floor is there are no gatherings of testosterone fuelled young men with their mates and beer jugs in hand; you know, like there used to be when you were... umm... old enough to visit a pub or club, all those years ago – when you were 16 pretending to be 18. What's happened? Where did all those young men go?

Some women may be lucky enough to find that perfect new partner on the dance floor; some may be introduced through friends. Not me, that was just not going to work. Then over dinner and a

What's the plan?

few wines one night, a dear friend introduced me to the world of internet dating. Not those 'Tinder' type sites that the kids play with and swipe one way or the other for a yes or no. She introduced me to real dating sites, the type that cater for the more mature, like us. Young enough to still be enjoying life, but old enough to have a wealth of life experience.

It looked easy enough; after you have selected a site to go on, uploaded a few nice photos, written about your hobbies, likes, etc. etc., paid a fee and clicked, you are online.

And so it begins.

Chapter 3

Tom, Dick or Harry?

There are multitudes of dating sites out there and they all offer to find you that perfect match. You know, like the little robot Dexter in the 1980s dating show *'Perfect Match'*. I wonder if Greg Evans created any real success stories from that show. I'm not sure if Dexter really helped or hindered possible love matches.

How do you know which dating site to join? You don't. If you are like me, you will take advice from friends who have been there and done that. Listen to their experiences.

Some sites are free to join; well this is until you sign up and then you discover if you want to see or contact potential matches there is a fee involved. Other sites let you know up front exactly how

Kissing Toads

much it's going to cost you for the three, six or twelve month deals. Some offer packages and some have special offers.

Here comes a new set of rules!

1. Check the sites out – make sure they are offering what you want.
2. Look at the joining terms and conditions.
3. Check what you are paying for and the length of the contract.
4. Make sure it addresses your safety as a user.
5. Make sure it is easy to use.

And then

6. Make sure you are comfortable using the site.

In the back of your mind, try to remember that old saying *'you get what you pay for'*.

Overall, most sites, well the sites I visited are pretty good. Some have lots of questions for you to complete. Others left the wording and descriptors up to you.

Remember to be careful because not everyone is honest, and yes, even scammers visit dating sites. When you get the first six hits on your profile all sharing what are supposed to be their profile photos and they look like super hunks or male models and funnily enough they all live in exclusive Sydney suburbs and they all talk about their undying love for you (even though you haven't met them), their messages are all very similar, then the alarm bells should be ringing.

Tom, Dick or Harry?

These super sexy studs are probably all the same little fat sleazy toad who is trying to catch you unaware and fleece you of whatever you may have in your bank account. These sleazes prey on vulnerable lonely women, so be warned and be careful. If you come across these toads report them to the dating site you found them on. As far as I am aware, all the dating sites have a contact point for reporting these sorts of findings.

So here comes another rule:

Rule # 7 – Be aware.

Nobody really likes rules, well I don't, but sometimes they come in handy. If only everyone's moral compass included honesty, integrity and transparency, we wouldn't need so many rules.

I don't really know where these scamming toads come from. They might really live in exclusive Sydney suburbs, but I doubt it.

Sadly, there are also some pretty good profile pictures that catch the eye but aren't always what they seem. Be aware. That eye-catching photo might have been taken ten years ago, or it might be a picture of a younger brother or a mate. I am sure there are women doing this too, but I'm not interested in looking at women's pictures. Overall, we should all be who we are, without pretences.

Kissing Toads

"You need a lot of luck to find people with whom you want to spend the rest of your life. Some people manage to find their soulmate. Others don't.
I think love is like a lottery."
Kylie Minogue

Chapter 4

Dating sites... What to say, what to do

I said earlier that these dating sites look easy enough, but are they? We are our own worse critics. No photo is ever going to be good enough. After all, I don't want to look prudish or pompous or too fat or too thin or too happy or too sad. Honestly, I don't know what I want to look like.

This is where friends come in very useful. They can be your biggest fan and most truthful critic. Use them, take their advice on board and then let your pictures tell the story of you.

Kissing Toads

Next is your written profile.
Let's see: -
- A little bit of history, my background.
- A blurb about my likes and dislikes.
- Favourite food, favourite wine.
- Movies, books.
- Sport, do I like to play or do I like to watch?
- If I like to travel or, am I a stay-at-home sort of person?

Don't talk about work and don't talk about income. You don't know who is checking out your profile. Some things are best left for the second or third date if you are comfortable, otherwise like me, talking income is taboo. That's my business. We will get to this later.

Be honest. Let your potential match know what you are looking for. It might be a happy ever after or it might be - I'm testing the water; it might just be a fling. **Honesty is everything.**

Do say if you are widowed or divorced, let's face it we are all on dating sites for a reason and for most of us, we have been hurt in one way or another and we are trying to be brave and heal and hopefully allow ourselves to move on and build a new future.

We are all looking for that almost perfect partner and we should make sure that we are clear on not settling for anything less. We want to kiss frogs, not toads. I think everyone knows the kissing frog's story has a happy ending, or maybe you don't know the story of the Frog Prince, but that's a tale for another day.

Dating sites... What to say, what to do

New Rule

Rule # 8 - Maintain your standards and don't settle for anything less. Rule #8 is really important and sadly, I almost let myself forget it.

I had a happy marriage to a wonderful man. I was a good wife – well, maybe even a great wife, an awesome mum and a fantastic grandmother. I'm fun, full of love and life. I enjoy life and I'm not going to change, so I need someone who will accept my history, then and now. These are my standard conditions.

Profile picture uploaded along with a pretty good profile, if I must say so myself. I scroll through the profiles that some whizz-bang computer algorithm has selected for me and then there were some I guess you call 'hits' to my profile from men on the site that know how to look for themselves.

Honestly, I had a moment of absolute... I don't know what you would call it, but my first algorithmic match just happened to be a good friend's ex -husband... oh no no no!

What's he doing here? After a few deep breaths, I calmed down. He is here for the same reasons as me but still it made me uncomfortable so I quickly removed myself from this dating site, my profile, pictures, everything about me. I had to make sure it all disappeared – I just felt so... embarrassed, I think is the word. Of all people, fancy matching me with someone I knew and didn't like. The only thing we ever had in common was we both liked seventies music.

Time to check out a different dating site, but I have the gist of things now so it won't be too hard to repeat the profile bits and pieces.

Kissing Toads

Okay! New site, terms and conditions suit me. Looks like a site I will be comfortable with, slightly different to the last, but hey I'm new to this and it was another recommended site from friends who have been there and done that.

Profile and pictures uploaded, so we start again. This site lets you know when people are looking at your profile. You get winks and you can get messages. I think a wink means they have noticed you, maybe put you on the back burner for later, or they might be shy and wait to see if you wink back. Others cut through the chase and just message. Sounds easy? Nevertheless, it is scary, particularly when you are new to all this.

I scroll through the profiles again, hmm interesting! Too old; too young. Does he really look like that? Why is he still living with his mum? GSOH, what's that? I soon learnt GSOH means *'good sense of humour'*. I didn't know that dating sites had their own set of acronyms. There is so much to learn here.

As you scroll through and read some interesting write ups, you think, do I believe what this man has written? For example, I was reading one profile that was supposed to be that of a bank manager, or so he said he was, but he couldn't spell and his grammar was atrocious.

There is so much data to get through, pictures, profiles, messages, and winks. Working out what's real and what's not; it really makes your head spin. This is harder than cutting out ingrown toenails.

Finally, some profiles look interesting.

There is just something about his picture or what he has written in his profile. He sounds like a good cook. He likes to travel. Aww! He has a dog.

Dating sites… What to say, what to do

Yep, this is looking good!

He is ticking boxes – and that picture!

He looks like the right age group. A bit sultry looking, a bad boy image comes to mind – nothing like Robbie Williams more like a Son's of Anarchy bad boy type.

(Remember the Golden Rule - *Rule # 1*)

It's time to make contact and see if there is a connection.

Different dating sites have different methods set up for making contact. You can send winks, waves, smiles, click the interested button or just send a simple message.

On this site, the message button was the go; after all, if you are interested, why not say something? Maybe suggest a coffee in a mutually agreeable, safe place. Hang on! You don't know if he is an axe murderer or lives in Bates Motel. New rule…

Rule # 9 – Your Safety is Paramount.

Stop, rewind! Before the coffee invite, perhaps a little dating site chat, just to get some idea of what he is like. Rules #7 and #9 come to the forefront of my mind; that is behind the nervous aspirations.

I start with a hello. My two-finger typing takes control and the words come together, a little lame at first, but my fingers and my brain are starting to connect.

'Hi there, I've just read your profile; we seem to have a few interests in common. Would you like to chat?' And then, click the send button.

Kissing Toads

Sounds like a piece of cake, easy, hey! Well, it's not. It should be, but when you haven't dated in a very long time, it becomes another one of those big steps that sits outside of your comfort zone and for some of us, it's a very brave step to take.

He will either respond or ignore; time to wait and see. He responds in the affirmative. So now what? Keep the conversation going? After all, he responded. In my case, the conversation was pleasant. We seemed to hit it off online, so this was good.

Before I have the chance to ask, he politely asks if I would like to catch-up for a coffee. He suggested I choose the location – this was good, makes me feel safe and then he asks if I would be happy to give him my phone number.

Don't you wish there was some kind of dating etiquette you should have learnt while growing up? Where are the guidelines on who contacts who and what is or isn't appropriate to say in that first message, any message?

Well, message sent, contact made and not quite ready to give my phone number, after all we haven't met.

We continued talking and quizzing and questioning each other online through the dating site. It was a good, safe starting point. Did I feel comfortable? Yes. Did he sound nice? Definitely, do I really want to catch-up? Certainly do!

Chapter 5

And so it begins

After the first few days of messaging through the dating site, we exchanged phone numbers. Was this the right thing to do? In my case, the answer was yes. I felt safe. He sounded lovely, and I trusted my instinct, my gut feeling; plus, I wanted to have a number in case I was running late or he got lost.

We planned the date night and over the next few days, we spent a lot of time talking on the phone and exchanged a few photos. While he had my phone number, it was way too soon to share my address. Rules #7 and #9 still apply.

Even though I had paid for a lengthy dating site membership, this man sounded like just what I had hoped for. I was hoping he was everything I had imagined, so for the time being, I stopped looking at the dating site.

Kissing Toads

Fingers were crossed that he would be what I had imagined him to be. I didn't really remember exactly what that was, but he was it!

Date night came around. The plan was to meet in a little coffee shop I had chosen. I picked one close to work, a little place where I knew the owners and I knew they would watch out for me.

As you would expect, or at least as I expected, the date was perfect. He looked just like his picture. I loved his deep husky voice, and he was easy to talk with. In fact, very easy. His hands trembled. He was so nervous. I was too, but it didn't show as much on me. He was what I visualised him to be.

We talked, and we talked. Coffee turned into dinner, the night just disappeared. We planned to catch-up again. In hindsight, I learnt that on those first few dates, you only hear what you want to hear. To me, this man was ticking all the boxes – so I thought.

Like any courting stage that you think is real, you only have time for each other and everything is just wonderful. You want to learn more about the other person and spend every spare minute with them. You want to know more about their likes and dislikes, family, friends, what they do for work, and what they do for fun. You look for commonalities, what makes them tick, what makes you both laugh. Do you like the same sort of movies, TV shows? The new discoveries seem endless.

I learnt my new man was a country boy. He had a few marriages under his belt. He had a family who I later met and fell in love with, but he wasn't into the friends thing. His previous life revolved around work and home, and home seemed like it was a very unhappy place.

And so it begins

I accepted that some men I would meet would more than likely be divorcees, as there are a lot of them out there. I didn't mind as long as they could accept that I was fortunate enough to have had a really good marriage. We had our ups and downs like everyone else, but we worked on making our marriage work. I don't think I could fully understand or appreciate the difficulties or unhappiness of a broken marriage.

He had never dated a widow but could accept that I had a happy marriage and, to his credit, we could discuss my life and loss. This was another box ticked.

We met each other's families – tick.

Intimacy was great – tick.

Long country drives, dinners, movies – tick, tick, tick.

Then it was time to meet the friends, or as I say, the extended family. Not so many ticks here. I noticed the rising anxiety levels and sensed how uncomfortable this was for him, but at the time I thought it was okay and he would eventually get to love my friends, just like I do.

Time moved along, life was good, I was happy. We both worked long hours, so weekend catch-ups suited us both. We spent a lot of our weekend time exploring hidden away little places. We had some amazing weekends away, and I was introduced to riding on a motorbike and car racing – who would have thought? It was all fun, and I was learning to enjoy life again.

We planned the holiday of a lifetime, saved for it and we did it. England, Scotland, Paris and Dubai. The places we visited were amazing. The holiday, well as beautiful as the places were; it was the first time in a long time I felt lonely – something wasn't quite right.

Soon, two years of dating had passed; I was still enjoying our weekend catch-ups. He suggested we make our catch-ups fortnightly so he could have time to do chores around the house and I could catch-up with my friends.

Note to self: Look for warning signs. Why doesn't he want to see my friends with me?

It took a while for the penny to drop and for me to realise that my friends couldn't be part of our life. They could be part of mine, but not ours.

So here I was going out with my friends and feeling like the third wheel. Here I was, supposedly in a relationship and going to dinners and shows with friends, but on my own. Here I was, breaking my own rules and making excuses for doing it.

The honeymoon was over, but I kept trying. I really wanted to make this relationship work.

We had our overseas holiday, but that wonderful thing called hindsight tells me that the holiday only happened because we had paid for it and we didn't want to lose the money we had spent. Well, that's my theory. The holiday was good, but it was like travelling with a work colleague. Anyway, we did it and explored some wonderful places and met some lovely people.

Reality was setting in and I knew this relationship was ending, but I still didn't want to give up on us that easily. I had always made things work, and I believed if love was the foundation, we could

And so it begins

work. I forgot that the love and the willingness to make things work had to be two sided, so after spending many of my visits on long walks and sitting in parks where I could have a good cry, I realised it was time to stop kidding myself.

The country drives stopped, visits with family diminished and fortnightly catch-ups moved further apart. I got in the way, or so I was told. There was no time for housework if he had to catch-up with me. Mind you, I spent most of those catch-ups on walks by myself or sitting in the rotunda in the park having a cry, so really I wasn't in the way. I kept asking myself what I had done. What did I do to deserve this sort of treatment? Or to be made to feel the way I did. I will never know what I did and I guess there are somethings you just have to accept happen for no reason, they just happen.

After two and a half years, it was time to say goodbye.

So here I was, 58 years old and on my own again. I wasn't bitter or angry. I felt a bit hurt, but what this relationship taught me is that I can fall in love again and it's okay.

Kissing Toads

"Sometimes it takes heartbreak to shake us awake and help us see we are worth so much more than we're settling for."
Mandy Hale

Chapter 6

Back to the drawing board

It takes a little while to get over a sense of loss, be it that most horrid loss –the death of someone you treasure or loss through separation, unhappiness or no longer being loved. Loss is loss, it's sad, and it's hard and it's lonely.

Some say loss is complicated, but what is complicated? Why is it complicated? To me, it's very black and white, its loss, it hurts, and it sucks.

It was time for some 'me time', time to grieve my loss, but also time to reconnect with the people who were always there for me. It was also time for me to take a good look at myself and what I had let happen to me.

Over the two and a half years, I hadn't realised I was losing the person who I was. I was distancing myself and making up excuses for accepting behaviours I normally wouldn't tolerate. This had to

Kissing Toads

stop. It was time to rebuild and let myself grow into the person I wanted to be - a stronger and wiser version of myself.

Three months later, wounds licked, big girl pants back on and I'm ready to revisit the world of internet dating sites and see who is out there. What have I got to lose?

Chapter 7

It's all about love and being loved

In her TED talk Marilyn Yalom succinctly describes her ideas on why the heart has become the symbol of love. I have borrowed some of her conclusions as the overall meaning to me is that love is very powerful and here's why:

> *The heart is a powerful organ. Its relationship with love goes back to the ancient Greeks, or even further. Philosophers agreed that the heart was linked to our strongest emotions, which of course include love.*
>
> *Plato argued for the dominant role of the chest in love and the negative emotions of fear, anger, rage and pain. Aristotle*

Kissing Toads

> went as far as acknowledging the heart as the supreme organ in human processes.
>
> The goddess Venus was renowned for setting hearts on fire. Her son, Cupid, fired the arrows and suddenly the heart was overpowered with love.
>
> The heart, it's our foundation for love. It's made love an important social value, an intrinsic part of being human.
>
> The heart is a symbol of love. It offers us hope and most importantly, it represents an ageless assumption that love can save us.
>
> https://ideas.ted.com/tag/marilyn-yalom/

As I said earlier, 'What have I got to lose?'

I know what it's like to fall in love, to be really in love. I know the way you lock eyes with your partner's. You feel connected and you go all warm and fuzzy inside.

Falling for someone, remember those days? The days you felt out of your mind. The dopamine kicked in and you felt like you were on another planet, – that's love.

Being in love means the other person is always on your mind. It's crazy and you can't shake it. The hormones kick in and the love drug phenyl ethylamine takes control. The infatuation is hard to break. I know, I know, chocolate has the same effect.

It's all about love and being loved

Love makes you happy. You want to be happy, and you want your partner to be happy too. This is really important when you are in love. Being in love has so much to offer and once you have been there, why would you not want to revisit?

So back to those dating sites, this time with more confidence and a determination to find my happily ever after.

Second time around I am remembering the rules and this time I will stick with them ☺

Well, this is what you tell yourself, but underneath it all the thoughts of rejection, what went wrong last time? What did I do? What do I have to do to get it right this time? All these thoughts and fears come back.

Then there is the big question. Can I do this again? Well, yes, I think I can.

Kissing Toads

"Being deeply loved by someone gives you strength, while loving someone deeply gives you courage."
Lao Tzu

Chapter 8

The finding love journey

Along the way, you learn so much more about dating and dating sites and once you are willing to open up and say you are on a dating site, you soon learn that there are a lot of women just like you also doing the same thing. All looking for love in unknown territory; some are even willing to share their stories and adventures from the dating sites; some good and some bad.

Along the way, I got to hear some awful stories of women who were all too trusting and were placed at great risk. Stories of women being taken to secluded sites and somehow managing to get away before the unforgivable happened. There are some very scary stories out there.

Kissing Toads

On the flip side, I have also heard stories that ended in marriage and happily ever afters. Overall, I believe there is still real love out there for those who want to find it.

I can't stress strongly enough, your safety is paramount – think back to the stranger danger messages we instilled in our kids. Always have a plan. There are a lot of good men out there, but there are also horrid toads that we somehow have to weed out and expose. Make sure you let your dating site know about any of your misadventures so we can try to protect other women from falling into the same trap that you might have experienced.

The good thing about talking with friends is you soon learn you can share your dating experiences with other women who know where you are coming from and who have shared the same or very similar situations.

Mentally, it makes a big difference to your wellbeing to have a friend to talk to, laugh with and to cry with. Sisterhood is important and sometimes the only thing that keeps you grounded.

Along my journey I was introduced to someone who, like me, has faced loss but for her more than once and she is also trying to piece her life back together again. Like me, she is looking for that Mr Right, someone to once again share laughing and loving and adventures and to feel safe with. We developed a strong friendship; it is really special to have someone to share with, who understands you and knows what you have been through within yourself.

The finding love journey

One day

someone will walk into your life and get it right where everyone else got it wrong.

One day
you won't have to wait for a call or a text back.

One day
you won't be the only one giving your all.

One day
you'll finally meet someone who wants to help you grow in life.

One day
you'll finally meet someone who isn't afraid to give "love" another chance.

One day
you'll finally meet someone you can trust with everything.

One day
you'll have your best friend, your biggest supporter, and your teammate all wrapped up into one person.

(Anonymous, n.d.)

Chapter 9

Finding another fish in the ocean

Dating site selected. I choose one from my last exposure to the electronic world. A site I felt safe with and it was easy to use.

Profile picture chosen, a happy head and shoulders shot that says; Hey! This is me.

Then the written profile:

About me

Here I am, now much more confident in telling a little of my story. Not too much, but enough to make sure any prospective connection knows what I am looking for. After all, I don't want to waste anyone's time and I don't want them wasting mine.

Kissing Toads

I'm happy to say I am widowed and trying to move on with my life. I want them, that is whoever is showing an interest in my profile, to know that I take nothing for granted, that I enjoy life and want to make the most of it. I also write that I want to share my life with someone who enjoys my company and who is aiming for a long term happy ever after.

My profile blurb also mentions that I enjoy my job almost as much as my family and friends, and I round it off with a couple of things I enjoy doing. I think that's enough to sum up who I am.

The dating site adds its own list of questions to answer. These are on the dating site to help probe a little deeper and to find commonalities with potential matches.

Questions like:-

- What do you do for fun?
- What is your favourite meal?
- What is the most interesting fact about me?
- Treasured possession?
- What is my most favourite place in the world?
- Who is my greatest inspiration?

The list goes on a little longer with a few more questions that may cleverly set the tone of conversations that follow.

It's funny that when you read your responses, you suddenly learn so much about yourself.

Time to find a few more pictures that support what I have written; and now time to upload. You don't have to upload evidence based pictures, that's just the researcher coming out in me. I am an evidenced based kind of girl!

Kissing Toads

Chapter 10

Getting off the dating roller coaster

There is much more to life than dating, and it's important to remember that. I am still a mother, a grandmother, a sister, an aunty and a friend. These roles are part of me. They make me, me.

All the people attached to my roles help me to be the person I am. They all have a part to play in keeping my feet planted firmly on the ground.

Wearing the grandmother badge is probably the best role in the world. A world of innocence, full of kisses and big hugs, fantasy, adventures and lots of laughs coming from cheeky faces with chubby rosy cheeks I just want to grab and smother with love. I love jumping in puddles, reading stories and kicking a football. I love watching these little people grow and develop; it just takes

Kissing Toads

you to a good place, a space where you can escape the everyday and just enjoy life because time doesn't matter.

Having sisters who enjoy a wine o'clock with you and who put up with your judgemental views on everything with no judgement on you is a blessing. One of my poor sisters was a great sounding board on everything dating. She endured my commentary on potential dating profiles, which I was constantly reading to her. Believe me, over a wine or three, it's really interesting what perspectives are debated over various profiles, including my own.

My sons, well, they weren't too keen on me dating. It took a little while for them to accept the fact that I was lonely and wanted to share my life again. They were very close to their father, and they soon understood that even for me, like them, no man would ever replace their father and the love we shared and I would give anything to have him back with me.

Reality is cold and cruel, so like me, they had to accept I was making decisions for my future, a future I didn't expect and could never have predicted. They did eventually come around. Both boys became very supportive and extremely protective of me.

Good friends are hard to find, but when you find them, you cherish everything they bring into your life and you hold them tight and keep them with you forever. You keep these people close. There are others too, people who come into your life as either a blessing or a lesson. These people also have a role to play in your journey, but they come and they go.

Back to the dating site! …

Getting off the dating roller coaster

Everything is uploaded. The dating site has approved my new pictures and what I have written. Yes, everything is checked before it's posted. Another safe guard, which is good. I am glad they screen everything intended for this site. It gives you some confidence in the thought that they are trying to protect you as much as they can from those sleazy toad types I mentioned earlier.

There are all sorts of toads out there and it's not always possible to be protected from them. **Remember rule #7 and stay aware!**

Kissing Toads

"Dating is different when you get older. You're not as trusting, or as eager to get back out there and expose yourself to someone."
Toni Braxton

Chapter 11

 # Meet the toads

The Urban Dictionary succinctly identifies a certain class of toads – *'those who will fuck you over any time they can.'* Seriously, they are out there not only on dating sites but everywhere and they are not all male - so please, please remember you need to be alert and trust your instincts.

I should point out that I am definitely not anti-male; actually, you already know that because I'm on a dating site hoping to meet the man who will sweep me off my feet. I want a frog, not a toad. I am still trying to believe that the right frog will turn into my handsome prince, just like the story books say.

Kissing Toads

Super toad hunters

Toads come in various forms. Beware of superannuation hunters, these toads are well versed in honing in on loneliness. They see it in your pictures and read it in your words. They know exactly how to manipulate you with their charm and, as the prize is worthwhile, they don't mind taking their time to get what they have come for. Remember, these toads aren't always online; they are out there in the manual world too. Be careful.

Often referred to as sweetheart scammers, they know exactly how to play the game, they know what strings to pull and they have been following you carefully. Social media provides them with all the information they need to make them seem appealing to you.

People often wonder how someone could be so foolish as to get involved with a stranger and give them money. It's simple really and can happen to people in any age group. With these toads, the game of deceit is easier to play with those who are most vulnerable, like widows or recent divorcees who are all particularly vulnerable to this type of manipulation of the heart. And it is not gender specific either; both men and women are equally targeted.

Unlike our everyday scammers, these toads come into your life and make themselves known. They aren't from some West African country. They are right here; expert conmen. These toads enter your life and become so entrenched you just can't live without them. Funnily enough, its family and friends who can sniff them out while you are too busy looking through rose coloured glasses

Meet the toads

making excuses to help them out and you don't want to know or accept what's really happening.

These toads are looking for a life on easy street. Most have nothing, no savings, no property, and no plans, that is; no plans until they met you. Fortunately, some women wake up to what's happening before their life savings have dried up, but for others; once he has access to your super or any other funds you have, he either helps himself to whatever he can, then disappears, or makes your life hell and things end up in a courtroom with him making a de facto property claim.

Be careful! You have worked so hard to build your superannuation nest egg. This money was to see you through the rest of your life and it can be gone in an instant.

Always question why that someone has come into your life. Do your homework. Ask yourself, what does a thirty eight year old male really want with a fifty eight year old me? Talking to him about his future plans is always a good start. Does he have a job? Who does he work for? What contribution is he making to this relationship? You need to know the answers to all of these questions. Check his Facebook page, meet his mates and don't give him access to your bank accounts; most importantly, listen to your friends and family as they are protecting you.

Kissing Toads

Tadpoles or toadlets

Do we call little toads tadpoles? Well, you can but I've learnt they can also be called toadlets. So, in this case, they will be called toadlets. Toadlets are the little boys, 17 to 19 in age (some are even a little older) who are playing on a dating site either for the fun of it, to get a laugh at your expense or thinking they can find their own Mrs Robinson and score with an older woman. Who knows what they really see in it? These toadlets stand out a mile, their messages, the words they use, poor spelling and grammar. You know them when you see their messages or they might respond to a message you have sent.

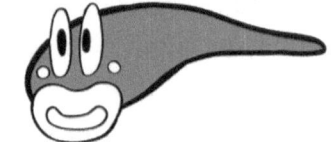

The first message I got from a toadlet was well written. There was no photo of him on his profile page. He had sent me a nice hello message telling me he had read my profile; yada, yada, yada; would I like to meet up? Somewhere in the yadas I could determine that he was just a boy, but the devil in me decided two could play this game.

After establishing he was in his first year at uni, lived at home with his mother and father, I then asked him why he was on an over 50s dating site. He smugly responded by telling me he wanted to know what it was like to be with an older woman. A smiley emoticon followed this. Here I did what any responsible mother would do. I asked him for his mother's phone number. On asking me why, I told him I wanted to share our discussion with his mother so she could see what her toadlet (oops!) little boy was up to. As you can probably guess; the conversation was over and I didn't hear from him again.

I got a few more odd messages from toadlets after this boy, but decided not to waste my time and energy on them.

Meet the toads

Honestly, there are all sorts of people on the world wide web, social media and dating sites and sometimes you are going to have contact with them whether you want it or not.

Scammer toads

Scammer toads are a bit like the superannuation hunters, but they want more. Their toad profile is the same as the hunters, but they could be based in Eastern Europe, Africa, or Russia, in fact anywhere in the world and they may not be little fat, sleazy, balding men; they could be women.

My introduction to this genre of toads came with a beautifully written piece from a man called Damon who somehow felt a *'warm connection'* to me. He told me that from reading my profile and viewing my pictures, he knew I would be interested in him. He amused me by telling me he could see I was a person of genuine feelings and emotions, not one of those women who wanted him for his looks and great body!

WHAT THE!!! Who's got tickets on himself? Mind you, I have to admit his profile picture, no shirt of course, showed him as what I can only describe as a WWF wrestler look alike – power packed and punchy! You guessed it; he lived in Millers Point in Sydney overlooking the Harbour (probably more so Croatia or Kenya) Anyhow never having experienced this sort of contact, I politely told him I wasn't interested, but thank you.

A few days later, I received almost the same message from what was supposed to be a different man. There were tell-tale lines about good looks and great body and guess what! He also lived in Millers

Kissing Toads

Point and looked like a WWF wrestler, just a different wrestler to my first encounter.

I responded to this guy. I asked if he knew the other guy, Damon, as they both lived in Millers Point and looked like they could be related. I also mentioned how surprised I was to receive the same message from both of them. I didn't get a response.

Making contact probably wasn't a smart thing to do, however I reported the two profiles to the dating company, and both were removed from their website.

The ACCC here in Australia has a really good scam watch page that is worth a visit.

https://www.scamwatch.gov.au/types-of-scams/dating-romance

On this page, they talk about how scammers take advantage of people looking for romance and how they do this through dating websites, apps or social media. These scammers pretend to be prospective companions; they play on emotional triggers to get you to provide money, gifts, or personal details.

The article goes on to talk about how scammers work, so in all of our interests, I have shared this information to help you protect yourself. Once again, **remember Rule #7. Be aware.**

> *Scammers typically create fake online profiles designed to lure you in. They may use a fictional name, or falsely take on the identities of real, trusted people such as military personnel, aid workers, or professionals working abroad.*

Meet the toads

Dating and romance scammers will express strong emotions for you in a relatively short period of time, and will suggest you move the relationship away from the website to a more private channel, such as phone, email or instant messaging. They often claim to be from Australia or another western country, but travelling or working overseas.

Scammers will go to great lengths to gain your interest and trust, such as showering you with loving words, sharing 'personal information' and even sending you gifts. They may take months to build what may feel like the romance of a lifetime and may even pretend to book flights to visit you, but never actually come.

Once they have gained your trust and your defences are down, they will ask you (either subtly or directly) for money, gifts or your banking/credit card details. They may also ask you to send pictures or videos of yourself, possibly of an intimate nature.

Often the scammer will pretend to need the money for some sort of personal emergency. For example, they may claim to have a severely ill family member who requires immediate medical attention such as an expensive operation, or they may claim financial hardship due to an unfortunate run of bad luck such as a failed business or mugging in the street. The scammer may also claim they want to travel to visit you, but cannot afford it unless you are able to lend them money to cover flights or other travel expenses.

Sometimes the scammer will send you valuable items such as laptop computers and mobile phones, and ask you to resend them somewhere. They will invent some reason why they

Kissing Toads

need you to send the goods but this is just a way for them to cover up their criminal activity. Alternatively, they may ask you to buy the goods yourself and send them somewhere. You might even be asked to accept money into your bank account and then transfer it to someone else.

Sometimes the scammer will tell you about a large amount of money or gold they need to transfer out of their country and offer you a share of it. They will tell you they need your money to cover administrative fees or taxes.

Dating and romance scammers can also pose a risk to your personal safety, as they are often part of international criminal networks. Scammers may attempt to lure their victims overseas, putting you in dangerous situations that can have tragic consequences.

Regardless of how you are scammed, you could end up losing a lot of money. Online dating and romance scams cheat Australians out of millions every year. The money you send to scammers is almost always impossible to recover and, in addition, you may feel long-lasting emotional betrayal at the hands of someone you thought loved you.

Scam Watch has some very useful information, and it's worth reading. They talk about protecting yourself, warning signs, what to look out for and what and how to report a scam.

We all want to feel loved and we all like people showing an interest in us, but we want it to be genuine. No matter how lonely you feel or how lost you feel, it is important to be aware and think with your head, not your heart, you have to protect yourself.

Meet the toads

There are a lot of good old-fashioned clichés to keep in the back of your mind and these two might help –

'If it seems too good to be true, it probably is.'

'Beware of the wolf dressed in sheep's clothing.'

It's surprising how many of us in our 50s live alone, particularly women. There is a lot going for having a place to yourself, especially when you can have total control over the TV remote and watch just what you want to watch or you can eat pizza in bed with a wine by your side or even chocolate cake and no one can tell you this is disgusting. Wearing your pyjamas all day and not feeling lazy; some people love it, want it, and dream about doing it, but not me.

My choice is to have someone in my life, to fight over the remote control – well compromise, at least. To enjoy a wine with a cheese platter for two while we cuddle up. To be with someone I want to be with.

For me, coming home from work should be about coming home to someone who is going to greet me with a smile and a warm hello hug and ask me how my day was. I know this isn't for everyone, but it's what I want and this is about me, isn't it?

Chapter 12

Beware of the wolf (Aka -hero toads)

I mentioned earlier to be aware of the wolf dressed in sheep's clothing. Nowhere does this ring truer than with the devious pursuing of older women. Ladies in their seventies or eighties or they may even look for some a little younger. There are some terrible stories of lonely vulnerable older ladies being scammed of everything they have, money, home and even dignity in what they thought was a second chance at love and marriage and even a new family to take on as their own. This same thing happens to older men too but is more prevalent with women.

Dorothy, an older lady I know, met what she thought would be her forever friend on Facebook. His profile and picture were that of a retired US war hero. Quite good looking for his age, lovely photos of his family, home and even his dog. There were even messages

Kissing Toads

on his page congratulating him on various acts of valour and service to his country. I guess you would say the all-round American hero.

Let's call this man Scott. I can't remember his real name, but Scott will do. Scott sent Dorothy a friend request. Dorothy, being an avid user of Facebook and someone who loved to make friends, looked at his Facebook profile and thought he looked good and sounded like just the sort of person she would like to meet or at least be friends with. He didn't seem to have many friends, one or two, so he was probably lonely.

Within minutes the first of many messages came through, a nice simple hello and a bit about how he stumbled across her profile and could see a glisten in her eyes that he thought would light up the room. He noted from her profile that, like him, she was a mature person who shared a lot of the same passions as him, so he thought he would take a chance and see if she would like to be a friend on Facebook. Dorothy was ecstatic, and so an online romance began.

The first few months were sweet messages just exchanging information about what's been happening in each other's lives, their children, grandchildren, pets, all of those nice simple topics that help you get to know a person better.

As time moved on the messages got a little worrying, Dorothy detected in Scott's messages that all was not well at home and even though he didn't say outright, she knew something was wrong so she was determined to find out what had happened and see if she could help.

Beware of the wolf (Aka –hero toads)

By now, Scott and Dorothy had been friends for over a year, so what could go wrong? Dorothy's daughter had raised concerns about Scott; she thought it was a little suspicious that this so-called American war hero was targeting her mother through a so-called friendship. After all, he lives in the US and they lived in Australia. So far, it seemed like no harm had been done. It was just friendly chats but, still as I continue to stress, **rule #7 - Be aware**.

Dorothy took offence at her daughter's comments and let her know in no uncertain terms that she didn't need her daughter interfering in her life.

Scott finally told Dorothy that things were not good, he didn't want to go into detail but he had lost a lot of money and was trying to figure out how he was going to pay his bills, he had an overdue car loan payment and it looked like his car may be repossessed.

As you guessed, without hesitation, Dorothy offered to pay and just needed to know his bank details and how much he needed. He then explained he hadn't paid for some time and the bill was $12,000.00 and it had to be paid before the end of the week. *Well, come in spinner!* The money was in his account that afternoon.

This happened a few more times, different little things like medical bills or one time he had said his daughter needed his help funding an operation for one of the grandchildren and each time Dorothy sent money. Before long, Dorothy was struggling financially. She ended up moving in with her daughter and explained that she would move out once Scott had repaid her.

With this, Dorothy's daughter tried to make her mother realise she was being scammed, but Dorothy wouldn't have it. She really believed this man cared for her; he was a good friend who had hit hard times.

Kissing Toads

Dorothy told Scott about her daughter's accusations. He was so upset he wanted to come to Australia and meet the family so he could prove how genuine he was. Not only that, but he also professed his undying love and told Dorothy he wanted to marry her (and of course she said yes). He just needed some help with the airfare.

Here we will put the brakes on and revisit what's happened. Dorothy is an 80-year-old female who lived on her own, happy with her life, her family and her pets. Life was simple, but lonely. Facebook was her communication tool, and she loved keeping in touch and meeting new people. Here she met a man who she thinks is in the same age bracket, shares her interests and her passions and she has fallen in love with him. He got into trouble so she is helping him out, as you would do for a friend (that's what she says!) and he is coming to Australia to marry her.

This dear lady, like I have mentioned earlier, is what they call a sweetheart scam. It's a typical playbook scenario where a scammer finds vulnerable targets in a particular age group, normally over 70, as they assume that they have more money to extort.

The scammer claims to be someone who seems like a hero, maybe a war veteran or a professional who has worked abroad. They exploit a victim's loneliness to quickly establish a bond and build an imagined future with them. They test the water with various tales of financial issues to see how much help their victim will give, and when they think they have them hook, line and sinker, they plan to meet up or, as in this case to come over and marry them but it all depends on the victim's willingness to part with money. Dorothy's daughter smelt a rat from the beginning, she had a gut feeling her mother was a victim but she couldn't get her mother to believe it, she tried involving the police but at this stage there

Beware of the wolf (Aka -hero toads)

was no proof a crime had been committed. The police offered to talk to Dorothy about what could be happening. To cut a long story short, Dorothy was fuming and left her daughter's home, as she felt her daughter was trying to destroy her one and only chance at happiness. Her parting words to her daughter were, *'Don't think you will get an invitation to the wedding. I won't have you there!'*

Dorothy now lives in a nursing home on a very meagre income. She lost all of her savings and her home. She refuses to see her daughter and still blames her daughter for destroying her only chance at happiness, even though Scott never showed up in Australia.

From reading the Military Romance Scams website, I've learnt that scammers like Scott spend a lot of time searching social media profiles and military websites for images of genuine soldiers. They then steal this information and use it to set up fake profiles across dating sites, social media and messaging apps.

Their next step is searching for vulnerable victims; more often than not, they target widows and older women who might be susceptible to their advances. Facebook is the perfect medium. Everything you need to get started is there in print. A ready-made worldwide pool of victims.

Back to the dating site

Hmmm... time to visit my profile page and see if I have had any visitors, any winks or messages.

Chapter 13

Meet Stu

Lots of winks and a couple of messages. I think it's good manners to respond to messages first, as these people have taken the time to not only look at your picture and read whatever you have written in your profile, but they have responded with words.

The first message looked interesting for a first contact – I have to admit, no matter what anyone says; you look at profile pictures before you read any profiles. I know this is shallow but we do it – there has to be an initial attraction, says she, the non-therapist!

I'm in position for first contact. Profile photo is appealing (sorry, but it has to be!)

It was nothing ground breaking, just a, 'Hi Julie, my name is Stu, actually Stewart but my friends call me Stu.'

Kissing Toads

Okay Stu. Well, it sounds like I am automatically classed as a friend. Obviously, he has read my profile. I read his. I noted he lives close by – big tick. Enjoys movies and dining out – tick and tick and the picture isn't bad either, so another tick there.

The profile write up is great when people take the time to do it properly. You learn a lot about a person from what they write and how they write it. I learnt he isn't a WWF wrestler from Millers Point, so that's a good start. Nothing obvious to refer to Rule #7 about, thank goodness.

A few more messages through the dating site and then we agree to meet. The plan put in place - coffee in a ritzy little café where both of us need to travel. Well, a 10 minute drive if that, but it is in neutral territory. We made it a post lunch catch-up and sat outside where we could watch the sea. What I didn't factor in was it just so happened that a national junior surf lifesaving competition was being held on the beach we were to sit above, so parking and seating were a nightmare.

Fortunately, I arrived early and could secure a table before one of the visiting competitor's families thought about taking advantage of the sea views from the well-placed table.

Shortly after securing the table and ordering a wine, Stu arrived. He looked quite dashing (as a Bronte sister would say!) and appropriately dressed for a first date at a beachside café.

Presentation is everything. One of the first things you look for is the effort a person makes when they are meeting someone new. In fact, you expect a person to make an effort, no matter who they are meeting or how many times you

Meet Stu

have met. Turning up looking sloppy would have portrayed a poor image, and alarm bells would have rung. In saying this, there are still well-dressed toads who like to portray a good image, but underneath it's another story.

Conversation started flowing as it should. The ice was broken. It was my first date in three months, or I should say my first date since licking my wounds after my last relationship ended, and it felt good.

Being outside, enjoying a sunny day at a lovely café, what more could you ask for? The nearby road was busy. I noticed that every time a motorbike roared past, Stu's attention was easily diverted. So as any reasonable date would do, I turned the conversation to bikes, not that I know much about them but it gave him the opportunity to focus a conversation with me. We finished our rendezvous on a friendly note with a second catch-up planned; dinner and a movie.

Date one was good, well, okay. He seemed nice, but nothing exciting. Actually, that sounds awful, but I really wasn't excited by him. No heart flutters or feel good endorphins. Maybe I was being a little tough on him, or even myself. I had just failed at what I thought was a great relationship. Even though I hadn't really failed, my confidence had taken a bit of a hammering, so I was mentally challenging myself here. Anyway, I was determined to give it a go, and he was the one who asked me out so he can't be all that bad.

Date two comes along. Dinner at a local pub followed by a movie of my choice. Might I add, he was the perfect gentleman. Yes, they exist. We talked and talked over dinner and he drove me home after the movie, seeing me safely in he then drove away. Again, what a gentleman.

Kissing Toads

On saying our goodbyes, we talked about catching up the following week. The whole night was just perfect, so I was really looking forward to our next catch-up.

The next week came and went and no call, no message. The week after came and almost went, but I thought bugger it, I will ring him.

I called, after the polite niceties – hello, how are you? How was your week? His response started off with something like. 'Sorry for not calling. I decided not to pursue this relationship any further.'

Left feeling stunned. What do you say? Remaining composed and totally cool on the surface, I just responded with, 'okay, thank you for telling me and I really enjoyed our first two catch-ups.'

The end! Just like that, it was over. It was time for a good cry and to feel miserable for ten minutes, and then it was time to move on. In one quick lesson I learnt, matches won't work all the time and its best to be honest, if you don't feel it – it's not going to work and if he makes it clear that he is just not that into you; end it kindly before either of you gets hurt.

It was around this experience that I thought there should be some form of etiquette associated with dating or even ending a date before it begins. I have mentioned this before, but I haven't yet found a Ladybird book or something produced by Penguin, something like their Book of Etiquette – *The Complete Australian Guide to modern manners (Alderstein, 2007).*

Meet Stu

Why isn't there a guide to dating?

Why isn't there a complete guide to Australian dating? Not the dress to impress, don't drink too much (really!) and don't talk about marriage or children.

Why isn't there something written about

- The etiquette of replying to messages online.
- Planning a catch-up – particularly that first date.
- Keeping in touch.

Or even

- How to end it before it starts.

Dating in your fifties is not like being sixteen again. Actually, I don't think I would like to be sixteen again, even though it was easier.

Google is a fantastic tool – well good for a laugh when you want dating advice, yes you can ask Google anything and it will have an answer.

So here we go, I asked Google

- Who should pay on the first date? I want to get this right as I'm out of practice, any advice I can get will be helpful. ☺
- What should you not do while dating?
- What date should you kiss?
- How many dates before you should sleep together?

Kissing Toads

While scrolling through Google (wine glass in hand) I also learnt that there is a five date rule and a ten date rule which I shall suggest you look up yourself.

For those like me who would like to see some rules out there, not that we really pay much attention to them, but we still know we need some sort of guide. It's good to know that even Google has some dating rules you can refer to; they are just not in a book. They aren't put together like a complete package of dos and don'ts.

As I was scrolling through all the Google Questions and Answers, which by the way should become known as the electronic Martha Stewart, I came across a question I hear all the time - Why is dating so hard nowadays?

Dating is harder because it's so common to look for what's wrong with a person instead of focussing on what's right. We expect an intense spark to be there from the start. If it's not, we check out and look for someone else because we think it's easy to meet someone thanks to modern technology.

There's quite a page on the web put together by Griffin Wynne (June 2019) that helps understand why we make dating so hard, it's worth a read: https://www.elitedaily.com/p/heres-why-dating-today. Thanks Google ☺

Meet Stu

"Never ever settle. You may think you aren't gorgeous, smart and have too many insecurities to count, but there is going to be someone in the world who truly loves you for you. Don't ever think that you have to put up with some man's shit because he is the first one in a long time to show some interest. You are beautiful in your own original way so never lower your standards."
Awesome Love Quotes

Chapter 14

How to watch for Red Flags

> 'The longer we ignore red flags,
> pretend they don't exist, the more
> we disconnect from ourselves'
> **Sherrie Campbell**

We have all heard of red flags and we know they are a warning, so why do we choose to ignore those early warning signs? Why is it that when the head says, 'this is not okay,' we look for excuses to make it okay? So many of us make excuses for behaviour we would not normally tolerate and if it was a friend in this situation, we would definitely point out the warning signs, so why do we not protect ourselves?

I must admit even I am guilty of this. The warning signs are there, but we want so badly for things to work out we overlook and turn a blind eye to those telltale signals that are flashing before us.

Kissing Toads

We tell ourselves, *'its early days, let's see how things go,'* or, even worse, we question our own judgement. *'Am I being too picky?'*- *'Am I focusing too much on what is wrong rather than what is right about this man?'*

In the early stages of dating and getting to know the new Mr Right, we forget to take off the rose coloured glasses. We see that, *'I only have time for you,'* as he really wants to get to know me and not as, *'why is he isolating me from my friends?'* Putting down previous partners, were they really that damaging or is it really him that was the villain and not the victim?

When he outlines his priorities, which look really good – work, family, travel, then sport - and you suddenly realise that you are not on the priority list, so where do you fit in? It's here you should question how important are you in the bigger picture of you and him? Is there any actual future here? I doubt it.

As women, we are very good at compromising. After years of bringing up children, we become experts in the field. Why is it now, in a new relationship, we find we are compromising to keep another adult happy – if you can call it that? We are doing all the things he enjoys and putting it down to him wanting to share his passions and this is okay, but it's only okay if it works both ways. After all, you have passions, things you enjoy and would like to share. If it's not working both ways, alarm bells should ring and a red flag should wave madly in front of you.

There are multitudes of red flags we grow to recognise, lying, aggression, mood swings. The list is endless. Keep the rules in mind. Be aware. Set the boundaries, the deal breakers physically, emotionally, and sexually.

Chapter 15

And now for the other toad

So far I have mentioned:

- The superannuation hunters
- The toadlets
- The scammers

Then there are the other awful subclass **Toadflingers.** What are these you may well ask? Toadflingers are the married men just wanting someone to play with on the side. Men with no respect for themselves; their partner or you.

Some at least have the decency to tell you up front they are only here to play, they are just looking for a good time and others, well they just string you along because you are nothing more than a bit of fun for a short time.

Kissing Toads

Remember rule #8 and maintain your standards. You are better than this.

Slimy, condescending bastards need their dicks cut off. I guess you can tell I don't like these toads one iota. Yuk! Yuk! Yuk!

I have seen profiles of these toads on dating sites. At least the ones I have seen have included within their write up what they are about. *'Fun loving middle-aged man looking for a fun loving lady who is here for a good time, not a long time.'* I think you get the gist.

I obviously don't like it, but there must be women out there looking for these sorts of encounters – not me!

The other term I have heard referred to in these situations is a 'Hall Pass'. In this situation, the couple have agreed to and given permission for each other to have sex outside of their relationship without consequences. It's supposedly a one off or some sort of temporary arrangement.

Personally, I don't know why people do this. I couldn't. Sex, being with someone, supposedly loving someone, for me is a commitment made with just one significant other. I don't see a relationship as a game or a bit of fun. Maybe I'm old-fashioned, but I would like to think that the person who has given himself to me only wants me.

It may work for some women, but not me.

I had one of these Toadflingers contact me, but he was polite enough to tell me up front what he wanted and to correctly mention that I would probably run a mile rather than meet up with him. I responded to his astuteness, and that was the end of that story.

And now for the other toad

I really think we need the *Modern Mature Aged Dating Etiquette* book.

But to get you started, remember :-
you can make first contact with a potential dating candidate if:

- Your gut instinct tells you it's okay.
- You see some potential worth exploring.
- You maintain your standards.
- You keep your safety as your number one priority.

Chapter 16

Meet Pete

So here I am, scrolling through the dating sites once again. It might seem sad that I'm in bed early on a Friday night with the television on and a white wine on the bedside table, no chocolates, cake or pizza. Just me, my wine and the television, oh and my phone. I forgot to mention my planned entertainment for tonight during the television commercials would be scrolling through the dating site.

Twenty-seven, no twenty-eight new messages on my profile page all awaiting my attention.

- Hi lovely, my name is...
- Hello gorgeous, want to catch-up?
- Hi there, looking for someone to make your day?

Kissing Toads

> In my dating book 'Modern Mature Aged Dating Etiquette' that is to be maybe one day on a bookshelf or even in e-book format, I would advise that on receiving a message from a potential suitor, one should always respond politely informing the potential suitor of your desire or of no desire for further contact. Well, as I am not Charlotte Bronte, I probably would not have been so formal in my advice, but what I would try to say is that good manners are everything!

It goes on and on, well, at least twenty-five more times.

Anyway, back to my messages. There's one that's caught my attention. His profile picture is eye-catching – an attraction hit! Like me, a widower, he has adult children, a businessman, lives quite some distance away, but that's okay. Time to make contact with a friendly hello text. Within minutes, I get a message back asking if I would like to chat.

It's Friday night, bed, tele and wine, yes a chat is a welcome addition to my exciting night! Why not?

Our chat was great, relaxing and with lots of questions about each other and our journeys through grief. He lives almost eighty kilometres away, but in real terms, that's not too far. We talked away most of the night and into the early hours of the new morning and planned a Sunday afternoon catch-up.

So far, so good! I learnt he was very active in his community and had just taken up dancing – this is all sounding good.

Meet Pete

Sunday came around and sticking to what I will call my modus operandi we met at the café I like to meet at, the same one where I met with Stu. We sat outside where we could watch the waves. Again, the rules - nice and safe.

Pete arrived; yes he looked like his profile picture, just a little shorter than I imagined. He was my height and I'm not tall. He was pleasant, a great conversationalist, and his conversation was with me and not distracted by every passing car or bike. We found lots to talk about. It was a fun meeting. As the afternoon rolled on and it cooled down, we sat inside and had dinner together.

More talking, lots of laughs and we discovered a lot we have in common. It was all just perfect. As the night came to a close, the bill arrived. Pete took a pen from his pocket and then proceeded to work out how much was his share and what was mine and, after putting his money on the table, he gave me the bill to check so I could pay mine.

Now I'm a modern independent woman and I don't mind at all paying my own way but just the way this was done took me by surprise. I was more than happy to pay or pay half. It's just the way he handled the situation that astounded me. I will have to come up with something about paying for meals in my book on Modern Mature Aged Dating Etiquette.

Other than this incident, it was a nice date, a great afternoon and evening, and he was a nice man. I hadn't had so much fun in a long time. And yes, a second date was planned.

Kissing Toads

Date two: To cut a long story short, flowers, wine and a lovely restaurant, no working out the bill - he paid! Things are looking better.

Date three was planned, but we had a bit of a hiccup in between. I had to go away for a few weeks. Sometimes things happen that you need to deal with or be part of and when it involves family, well, that comes first, so a raincheck was promised for the third date and off I went.

While I was away, there were several text messages, calls and photos sent between us. I really appreciated the interest he was showing in me. We still didn't really know much about each other, but it was nice to have someone who wanted to keep in touch even though we had only just met and we were hundreds of miles apart.

Our long distance contact was going really well, that is until... I asked to see photos of his family. He sent me photos of both of his children and I sent him photos of mine.

The message I got back was a little disturbing, well it was to me. In comparing the photos of our children, he responded with a text telling me his children weren't as good looking as mine. Being a very proud mum, I agreed with him but I would be the same with any other pictures of family too, I love my boys and I think they are the best looking blokes around but as a dad he should have been proud of his kids and their looks after all he helped produce them! Not a good response, but hey not an issue and I let it go.

Things were going well. It was great learning so much about someone and feeling very comfortable with what I was learning about him. As the days progressed, he sent me photos of his home, spoke more about his hobbies and being involved in his community. It was all sounding good, promising.

Meet Pete

After my few weeks away, I arrived home. It was time to get some sort of normality back into life. We arranged date number three, and this time it's for the weekend! We made plans, dinner, a movie, a sleep in and breakfast. Sounds perfect doesn't it?

Well, it should have been a perfect weekend. Dinner was nice; movie was great but conversation, honestly! The things people worry about. Why did I have such good-looking kids? How was it my marriage worked so well and then to be told it's not fair that I had things so good when others – I think he meant himself just couldn't find that same happiness? As he went on, all I could hear was resentment for everything in his life.

This is when you have to make it clear that the conversation has to stop. I let him know it is sad his life was not so happy and yes, I was lucky and yes, I am blessed with a beautiful family (inside and out). It's time to move on to a new conversation, or maybe another glass of wine. The night was becoming a fizzer.

I don't want to sound mean, but I'm not a counsellor and I didn't know his wife who had passed away, and his kids looked okay to me. They had both excelled in their careers; I honestly didn't know what was going on. I didn't want to be dragged into all of this negativity. Life had been cruel to both of us. We had suffered pain that will always be with us – well, it will for me, but never the less I have wonderful memories to hold dear and a family who I cherish.

Maybe his marriage was not so good and maybe there was a rift with his kids, but that had nothing to do with me. As hard as it is, he had to move on and make the most of what life he has and funnily enough, from our earlier conversations, that is what I thought he was doing.

Kissing Toads

This was the end of our night, and as I said earlier, the night became a fizzer. It was time he went home, but he didn't. It was late and a long drive, so I let him sleep... in the spare room.

I should have asked myself what I was doing. Someone who had sparked an interest was quickly showing me a side of him I was starting not to like. Where is my rule book?

Sunday morning, the sun was shining. I still put myself out and made a delectable breakfast, if I say so myself. Breakfast and my efforts didn't change a thing. There was still a sense of, I don't know, but a sense of something resentful and miserable in the air. I think someone had a lot of issues to work through.

As he left, his parting words were that he had never ever been treated as well as I had treated him and he found that hard to deal with. He left shortly after that and we had agreed he could call me again soon.

Chapter 17

One of life's greatest treasures

'Good friends help you to find important things when you have lost them – your smile, your hope and your courage.'
Doe Zantamata

Life was getting back to normal.

One of the latest things I had reintroduced into my life was dinner catch-ups with friends. This had become a weekly event. Our dinner party of two soon became four. Four women who could get together and share stories, laugh, cry, be silly – you name it, we could do it because what was said at that dinner table stayed at that dinner table. More on this later!

Kissing Toads

Now remember, I mentioned earlier one of the most important things you can have is friends. Perhaps I should create a list of things you should have in your dating toolbox, and near the top of those items in the box would be your friends.

Friends - The people that have your back no matter what. They are around through good times and bad.

Husbands die or can leave. Significant other halves come and go but real, female friends, they are your rock. They are always there. They are your biggest critics and biggest supporters. They love you to the moon and beyond, so yes, they are the top item in the dating toolbox.

I haven't spoken about toolkits or what should be in your dating toolbox yet, but everyone needs one and you will find everything you need to put in your toolbox for future use as you work through the world of dating.

Life for me is in boxes. This is how I mentally keep things in order. And please don't take offence, but I do this with my friends as well – it's how I cope, how I deal with life. The lids are kept open on most of the boxes. I just like everything neat and tidy.

I have a very special friend who I met through my husband and she is like a big sister. I keep her in a special box. My friend and her husband keep me grounded; they are always there when I need them. Always have been and always will be. This may sound strange, but their okay with potential suitors means a lot to me. Their approval is important. I owe them so much. The love and

One of life's greatest treasures

support they gave me and my family through dealing with the cancer and losing my wonderful husband is a debt I can never repay.

In another box I have my school mum friends – strong independent women who have all faced their own challenges and remained strong and tight-knit. These women are incredible and they are fun and know how to make you laugh when you need to.

Lots of boxes to unpack here. I just hope they all fit in the toolbox, which I am pretty sure they already do!

Next, I have a dear friend who, well, I like to say, is my accomplice when it comes to trouble. She is, to me part of my family, always there and kicks my butt when needed and she is very lucky to have the husband that is the persona of an almost perfect husband and like my other friends I have already acknowledged she is always there for me, especially when I have had one too many.

My next group of friends I will call season two. Two kids, two groups of mum friends. These ladies are treasures, strong women, more of a 'sisterhood'. We have shared the joys of teenage years and football and whatever crazy shenanigans our boys got up to. We have also shared the tears of loss and held our boys together when they shared the tragic loss of a friend. These women have shared every up and down with me – the joys of being a football mum, rebellious school issues, health issues, death and me getting into the dating scene. These women also wear the badge of family.

Along the way, I was introduced to two other women, who, like me, were on their own and looking to see if they could find love again.

These ladies were made known to me through those weekly dinner nights I spoke about earlier. Those dinners became my salvation for

Kissing Toads

a while; they helped me regain my confidence. We soon introduced what we called a 'cone of silence,' translated, this means what is said at the dinner table stays at the dinner table. I think I will add a cone of silence to the toolbox!

On these Wednesday night catch-ups, we enjoyed a meal over a few drinks and we laughed and we cried and cried even more over our losses and our new experiences. One of these lovely ladies taught me a new rule which really helped in tumultuous times between relationships, *'an ex is an ex for a reason'*. This, my friend, refers to my first so-called success on the dating sites and a few in between. This lovely lady has become a real BFF. We have so much in common and we have become great supports for each other.

It just so happened one night at dinner, the weekly catch-up, cone of silence dinner, I was asked how things were going with the latest interest from the dating site – you know the one who had problems with my kids being better looking than his! This may seem really weird but it's true, as I was responding to the question saying that I didn't know as he hadn't contacted me since our weekend together, which was over three weeks ago; my phone beeped, well it made that funny noise you hear when you have a message and sure enough, it was him. It was just a short message asking how I was.

How uncanny! It was a nice surprise as apart from his minor hang-ups, he is actually a nice person. I was on my way to saying that I thought the relationship was over before it began, however, maybe I was wrong.

In line with the good English, catholic school girl grounding I've had; I politely responded. I mentioned in my message that I was just talking about him and reassured him it was all good. After all,

One of life's greatest treasures

I didn't want him to worry about what I might have been saying. No response.

Dinners with friends are so therapeutic. What is said during the dinner conversation stays in the dinner conversation. The good thing is, while you are busy feeling sorry for yourself, you soon learn others have similar stories and some stories are worse than others. It's good to share and walk through the events of what did or didn't happen.

Rejection, bad behaviours, and left hanging on the edge can be very hard to carry on your own. You need to talk things through and sometimes you need help to reboot your confidence and be reminded of who you are.

Like me, my BFF has dealt with a series of disaster dates; however, hers were more nightmare dates which can be a real blow to your confidence. I can't understand how my stunning, beautiful friend, beautiful inside and out, finds so many drop kicks. Like me, she had a marriage made in heaven, her own perfect world that, in the click of a finger, changed. As I said earlier, life sucks.

Like me, she just wanted another chance at a near perfect life. She just wanted to find someone who wants to share a wine and some cheese in front of the television on those cold winter nights, someone who could love her unconditionally for who she is and someone who would make her feel safe.

My gorgeous friend seemed to attract those toads that made her feel sad, worthless, and they took away her confidence. My friend, like the rest of us, is better than that and no man has the right to make her or any woman feel that way. Everyone deserves to be loved, respected and to feel wanted, cared for and safe.

Kissing Toads

As a dinner group, we were really good for each other, but this one lady, my friend, shared so much of what I had gone through, we just connected on a different level.

Divorce is nothing like death, so having someone who understands the emotions you have to work through of being in love with someone you no longer have, shedding a tear when your together song comes on the radio or when a memory jumps to the forefront of your mind is not something everyone can relate to.

We could laugh and cry at the same time. We could share stories of the loves we cherished and how they made us feel and we reaffirmed between us that under no circumstances were we about to settle for second best. We knew what it was like to be loved and respected and we wouldn't settle for anything less.

Back to Pete

Well, a week after the dinner and still no response, so time for a friendly message just to touch base and see how he was. After all, he initiated the contact last week and just left me hanging there, not knowing where we were going.

I asked how he was going and what he had been up to and if he was still involved in his dancing. He politely responded shortly after getting my text, just saying, *'yes I'm fine and getting much better with my dancing'*. No hello, how are you or what have you been up to? No, nothing.

I can proudly say I got the message; this relationship was over. I realised I wasn't really that important. It seemed like his other interests were far more important than a quick hello call or a message to me.

One of life's greatest treasures

Let's chalk this up to what I can now call experience. Experience has taught me it's not always going to work out. People all have different expectations, and experience has made me stronger. I didn't cry a million tears or question what I must have done wrong. I am now strong enough to realise that sometimes it just doesn't work – it's over!

As they say, back to the drawing board or, in my case, the dating site. I spent a bit of time just scrolling through profiles, looking at pictures and reading messages, but I wasn't really in the mood to put myself through any potential interests at the moment.

No matter what anyone says, dating is hard work, it's emotionally taxing and for those of us from the old school it's something we take serious it's not a game; there are feelings and emotions at stake.

It's times like this where you feel you need to close off for a little while and just spend some time with yourself or time doing things you enjoy, like catching up with friends. There is nothing like a glass of wine with a friend while watching some silly reality TV show. Honestly, you can share so much and gain a whole new insight on life watching Married at First Sight!

Kissing Toads

Chapter 18

The lonely hearts club

There is another group on the dating site I haven't mentioned yet and they aren't TOADS and with their attitudes and values, they could have been and probably once were someone's handsome prince.

This group I describe as the very lonely older men, gentlemen in their 80s, who might be looking for that last grasp of love or companionship in their twilight years. More so, I think these lovely men just want someone to talk to.

Loneliness can mean many things to many people. It can be social, and it can be emotional. The impact of feeling lonely can have a tremendous effect on our mental health and well-being.

Loneliness can affect people at any point in their lives. Have you ever found yourself in a room full of people and still felt isolated? That's loneliness. Have you ever put on the brave, shall I call it 'life

Kissing Toads

of the party' face, but deep down, you just want to cry and have someone hold you? Again, that's loneliness.

Retirement, redundancy, loss, be it through separation or death, it all brings about loneliness.

Emotional loneliness happens when that someone special is no longer in your life. A particular risk group is these older men. They have been husbands, fathers, and breadwinners and were connected to a community and a family and now, in what should be their golden years, those years that should be spent sitting on the porch watching grandchildren play, they are alone. Women face this problem too; however, women are better at keeping that social connectedness, and unfortunately a lot of men struggle here.

Connecting with lonely older people can be good for you and for them. When you do this on a dating site, just remember you need to have some rules in place. I know, I know, I am constantly introducing new rules, but as I keep saying, rules are important; particularly when you are connecting with a lonely person. Remember, they are vulnerable too, so being kind and caring and honest is important.

You know why you are on a dating site and you know what you want, well hopefully you do; it should all be in your profile – you know that blurb you put together with a photo or two.

Sometimes amongst the messages on your dating site page, you might scroll across a lovely message from an older man who might just make a flattering compliment or it might even just be a friendly hello.

There are two choices here; one, you can either ignore them and scroll to the next message or two, you can thank them for their

The lonely hearts club

compliment or just say hello. Sometimes the thank you is the end of the conversation and other times it can be the start of a conversation that might go on for a little while. The conversations can be more like a father and daughter thing than a looking for love conversation. It's important that intentions are made very clear at the start if you want to continue with friendly chats that aren't meant to go anywhere.

A friendly hello, how is your day going? Or even asking how the dating site is working for them can just make an old man's day and give them a source of connectedness.

So, the unwritten rule here! Be friendly but careful not to build a relationship you don't want to commit to. Share a laugh or two about some of your dating decisions and know when it's time to say goodbye and move on.

I never really understood loneliness until I had my heart ripped out after thirty four years of marriage to an incredible man. I was and still am very lucky to have two incredible sons and amazing friends and as loving and as caring as what they are and I truly appreciate it all; that sense of loss, hurt and loneliness was there for a very long time.

The loneliness of not having anyone to hold you or tell you everything will be alright. Losing dinner for two; the slow, sometimes silly dancing, and twilight walks along the beach and even the disagreements and making up – how you miss it all when it's no longer there.

I am my own person and always was, but that attachment, that special bond you have with someone you love and cherish, when it's gone, it is a horrible, lonely feeling.

Kissing Toads

Some may say chatting on a dating site with people for the sake of just a chat is a waste of time, but not me. It's not for everyone, especially when you are on a mission and that mission is to find love, but sometimes, slowing down and talking to others out there for the sake of a friendly chat, no strings attached, is another form of therapy.

I met two older gentlemen on the dating site; I loved talking with them through our messages on the site. They would tell me about their families, children, and grandchildren. They would talk about the women they had met but just couldn't hang on to, their previous working life and the wives who they adored and really missed. They had fought in wars and seen some terrible things, but losing the loves of their life was the hardest thing they had dealt with.

These were good men and deserved a second chance at happiness. I really hope the right ladies will realise what gems these men are.

Listening to their stories and picking up on their loneliness also taught me how vulnerable these people are. It made it easy to see how they could be taken advantage of and we know this happens, but I just can't understand how people can manipulate someone's loneliness for such mean and selfish reasons.

Chapter 19

Meet Tom

The electronic dating world is vast; it's overwhelming and can take you places you didn't think you would go. For me, that was taking an interest in someone with teenage children. Don't get me wrong, it's not that I don't like kids –I do; in fact, I love them but my children days are over. Mine grew up and left the nest. I see them, love having them around and I adore the grandchildren they have given me, but now it's my time.

I have had my share of cute babies and school sports and the Wiggles. It's now my time to enjoy being me and to do the things I want to do.

Time to check the dating site, again –

This man looks and sounds interesting and might be worth getting to know. I push the issue of kids to one side; for the time being anyway – why not?

Kissing Toads

A few messages on the site, he responds as I thought he would. Sounds really interesting. His views on social justice and what's going on in the world sound similar to mine. We compare our travels and views on world affairs and I like what I hear.

He politely asks if he can call me, and I politely respond in the affirmative. It's nice to actually talk to someone rather than letting my fingers do the talking.

Rules well and truly ticked, a catch-up is organised. No matter how good someone sounds, safety always has to be the number one priority, so it is a coffee by the beach.

By now, you have probably guessed that would be my next step. There is just something about the beach and the salty sea air, so a café on the beach is always on the cards with me and it doesn't matter which beach but for first dates it has to be one I feel very safe at.

I was on time, he was late. This is a popular beachside area so I guess being late is excusable, after all, parking is difficult. The coffee was good and so was the company. The time flew by and before long, it was time to go. He was having dinner with his children. We agreed we would like to catch-up again, maybe for dinner, and on that note, we parted ways.

Planning dinner wasn't easy, as it had to work around school and sport pickups. Remember the football mum, netball dad, whichever. They are priority tasks when these are your children. It was a challenge, but we made it work and planned our dinner date.

Another great catch-up. Again, he was late, not kids this time, but work. I guess that can happen when you work for yourself.

Meet Tom

The second date, they say, is when you learn more about a person. This is the time you get a sense of what they are all about.

First dates are scary; that is, according to doctor me. She with no counselling qualifications, just extensive experience; well, three or four dates anyway. The first date is full of angst, to me, on this date appearance and manners are everything and the mandatory tick box may get a tick in it, but its date number two where you look for substance.

Second dates are far more meaningful. We learn about each other's interests, passions, ideals and goals. Second dates show there is obviously an interest; we want to learn more about each other. For me, it's also a recheck on the first date. It's a recheck to see if that chemistry I first identified is real. Here is a chance to remove that first date anxiety and see what he is really like. Maybe there is a spark here, so it's the second date that we really put in the effort to see if this might work. Is it worth pursuing?

I read somewhere, probably online, yes it was online and worth a read on Cosmopolitan.com:

The blurb I read said *'seventy four percent of people actively looking for commitment will more than likely give a second date a chance. The more you get to know a person, the more you get to like them or you realise they are not for you.'*

Second dates get past that generic stuff, things get real. I might like you, but I might not.

I like real world, today stuff, so to impress me it has to be someone who lives in the here and now, who can hold a conversation on politics, world events, business and social justice – civil society

Kissing Toads

type issues. I can also take on conversations about movies, books, sport, cars; anything really if I sense a passion.

So here we were classy dinner, great wine, conversation boxes ticked and ticked again, and all of this without getting to kids and families. The night was going fabulously, but we both had to work the next day, so sadly it had to come to a close. We finished the night with a plan for date night number three.

They say the third date is all systems go, or YOU have been selected or it could also mean three strikes and you are out my friend! It all depends on how you look at things.

We humans are funny creatures. We use date number three as our yes or no number (so the experts say).

Date number three is the clarifier. It determines if this relationship is worth pursuing and kids aside, this man was ticking nearly all the boxes; interesting, engaging, shared passions and a gentleman. Everything was looking good, great even.

Dinner this time was a not so expensive restaurant, enjoying nice food that we discovered we both loved along with a good wine. This time the conversation was a lot more down to earth, realistic conversation about us. A type of conversation that implies without saying; what his priorities are and what they have to be. In a nutshell, life revolves around his work, work travel and his family. Sounds fair I guess as he is raising two older teenagers who are both active in their sports, and working for himself, his working priority is also a must.

Not sure if there will be a priority space for me in here but I'm happy to wait and see. I appreciate all the cards on the table – so far.

Meet Tom

We then move on to his passions, very similar to mine. All is sounding good and, as expected, we are planning catch-up number four. Still in the friend zone, but the attraction is growing and yes, kissing, even intimate kissing, is and was permissible. Kissing is important too.

By date four, you should know where things are heading. Three dates have gone well, a few text messages in between. Yep, so far, so good!

Date number four, a weekend date. All of our other dates have been after work, so it's been more a kiss and run, so this time hopefully a little more relaxed. Our plan: dinner and a movie and... see where we go!

It's Saturday. I'm sitting, ready and waiting. He eventually gets here. Poor man looks exhausted. Kid's sport, work commitments, and a few late nights in town with me. I can see it's taking its toll.

Dinner was great, and we both enjoyed the movie. In fact, it was one of those movies that lead in to those common interest discussions. Time for coffee and a little passion; all good, but then it ended a bit like the Cinderella story where he had to leave before turning into a pumpkin. No, seriously - kid's curfews to be met.

Here I was at the end of date four and really liking this man, who also seemed to really like me, but something didn't seem quite right.

A text through the week and date five is planned. There are never any guarantees you have found a potential long term partner or someone who will sweep you off your feet, but by date five you would think you would know where things are heading. Uh, uh not me!

Kissing Toads

It's a cautious yes, I really do like him, yes he is ticking all the boxes, but there is a **BUT** I can't put my finger on. Is it time to get serious? Hell no! Date five can be translated into eight or nine hours all up, so not time for this little black duck to be thinking serious at all and as I said there is a BUT!

Date five for me was a planned re-run of date four. Once again, I'm ready and waiting; and waiting... My date finally arrives, but a little too late for the movie we planned to see and hopefully we still have the table I booked for dinner. Fortunately, we could. Dinner was pleasant, but I could see he was exhausted, so our night fizzled out with him, saying goodbye and heading home for a good night's sleep.

I was starting to really like this man, but I wasn't sure where this relationship was heading. He had the same feelings about me, well so he said and I am sure that he believed our relationship was heading in the right direction.

The next few dates weren't really like dates, as I know a date should be. We had several after work catch-ups in town before he had to leave for dad duties and the BUT was still hanging over me.

A long weekend was coming. He had planned a trip away with his son and I had planned a weekend away with my grandchildren. A bit of escapism is always good, particularly with grandchildren. Lots of love and adventure and a differing perspective on life; much better than the bubble I had placed myself in.

I did text the lovely man I had been seeing, and he responded more than once, but I think it was time to burst the bubble I had put myself in, time to take off my rose coloured glasses and analyse the BUT hanging over me.

Meet Tom

Sometimes you can let yourself get carried away thinking everything happening is what should happen, even when it's not. I guess that is because you so much want it all to be right. It's here you have to wake up and question if this relationship is working. Is it really what you want it to be? Or is it that you are so lonely you are doing everything to try to make it work? Is it really what I am looking for? Is he really who I want to be with? What am I doing to myself?

Let's play fly on the wall and put things into perspective, or better still, start listening to that little voice in the back of my head that is telling me to wake up. That poor little voice has been doing somersaults inside of me, trying to make me face reality. Maybe I could use the excuse that the obsolete French and Latin words somersault or sombresautt had no meaning until now or maybe I was telling my inner self I was going to make this relationship work, even if it's not meant to!

New rule here, one that I won't give a number because we should all know it... **Use your common sense!**

I thought I had followed all the rules. Maybe I bent them slightly, but I didn't follow the most obvious unwritten rule, a pre-defined action we should all do and use common sense.

In my mind, I revisited each date and in doing this I found every alarm bell I should have picked up on earlier –

- I didn't want a relationship involving kids.
- I don't like people being late without letting you know.
- I was making excuses for his lateness and always being tired.

Kissing Toads

- It was made clear that his work and kids were his priority.
- At no time was it mentioned where I fitted into his life.

In thinking about the situation, I felt I was being used. I'm not blaming him as I let it happen because I was the one making excuses for him; excuses that I thought I could accept, but I really couldn't. What was I doing to myself?

Following my self-evaluation, I enjoyed my weekend with the grandchildren and didn't text Tom again. Funnily enough, he didn't text me either.

You might call this a waste of three months, but I think I might just call it experience; another one of those situations I should learn from. I learnt and I hurt from what I shouldn't do to myself. I didn't value my self-worth.

Life is full of things to learn, and each day I'm learning more about myself.

I'm learning –

- How strong I can be.
- To trust my instincts.
- That what I want has to be my priority.

I have also learnt how moments of weakness or even loneliness can take you where you don't want to be, but I now know I can get myself back on track.

Wow! I really like what I am learning about myself. I just have to keep practicing and applying these learnings to me.

Meet Tom

At this point in my life, I don't need a Dale Carnegie or Stephen Covey model of me. I just need to apply some common sense and be kind to myself. This is something we should all be doing, not as a rule, but as the right thing to do for you.

I spent so many nights questioning why I couldn't find my perfect match. I cried over stupid dates that didn't work. I tried to figure out what I had done wrong. I even spent time swearing at and cursing my darling husband, blaming him for leaving me to deal with all this crap, and then I would cry myself to sleep.

Chapter 20

It's not a crying shame

I still cry from time to time, but these are good, sad tears. It may be over a song we both loved or a song that meant something to us. Songs that would take you back to those special moments. I cry over significant days or when visiting places with special meanings, but there are no longer tears over dates that don't work. I am learning to accept some things aren't meant to be and if it's not what I want; I don't cry, I just let it go.

I am learning and accepting I am who I am and I will not accept second best.

I'm better than that.

Patience is becoming my virtue.

Chapter 21

Times are a changing, are you?

How times have changed! So far, I have introduced you to four of what I will call significant dates; that is those I saw as possible relationship potential and in one case I guess you could say it was a relationship. We will forget about the dates I think are best described as time wasters. These are the ones that fizzled before they even got started. The ones where you agree to meet and when you show up, you realise he is nothing like his picture so you make the quick escape before he sees you or the others where, on the first date your instinct smells trouble, he isn't who you think he is or it's not safe – time to leave ladies.

Remember the rule about your safety being the priority!

Kissing Toads

In the old days, it would have been said that there were names for women like me and yes, that's how it was. Women had heavy expectations placed on them. We were expected to grow up, get married, have children, and raise a family, and then what? A husband would die. You dressed in black and served a period of mourning and then remained a widow until the end of days.

Sometimes family would match you up with a potential second husband and this was probably done because some lonely man needed to be looked after and it also took some of the financial burden off the family. It wasn't about love or enjoying life. This was never seen as a requirement for women, particularly older women.

It's hard to believe how many steps forward Australian women have taken over the years to be recognised within their own right. To be recognised as a person, an individual who can make their own decisions and who is not someone's property but a strong, independent force that has and still is making their mark in what is still seen as a man's world.

Does anyone bat an eyelid at men who from a young age were encouraged to break many hearts or have so called healthy flings or count their conquests, which they would proudly skite about at the local over a pint or two?

Women who may have done the same would have been ostracised and, to some point, they still are, even when they haven't behaved like their male counterparts. Thank goodness some of us were brought up through the varying waves of feminism and we don't tolerate these kinds of behavioural views or beliefs.

Times are a changing, are you?

Why is it that women are judged? Why are different expectations placed on women? Why is it we had to have a #MeToo movement to bring attention to the deplorable behaviours of powerful men who demean and undervalue women?

It's not that long ago that there were some brave outspoken women who were described as ugly, vain, stupid, and greedy and often they ended up behind bars, yes, in prison cells for trying to get equality for all women. These women I describe as heroes amongst women, these suffragettes, our first real feminists paved the way for women, for women to vote, own property, gain strength and be recognised. These women were the first to say, 'it's not okay.'

Living in a country that was the second in the world to give women the right to vote and where one of its states, South Australia was the first in the world to also allow women to be elected to parliament (with the notable exception of First Nations women), why is it we are still judged and still feel like some man's property or play thing and not his equal?

As the song says, we are roaring in big numbers (see *Helen Reddy, 1972: I am Woman*) and yes, we are making progress, but in a truly civil society; which is what we are supposed to be - why aren't we treating each other with respect? Why don't we consider what each other has been through or what some are still living through? Why do we judge so harshly? Why can't we just be kind?

It would be wrong of me not to acknowledge that there are nice people out there; men and women, but for some reason a lot more of the mean, nasty and selfish people make themselves known while the caring and loving people out there are quietly getting on with life.

Kissing Toads

There seems to be many unanswered questions when it comes to dating and relationships and some of these questions just don't have answers, so maybe sometimes you have to park the question. You might figure it out one day or it might be easier to let it go and move on.

Chapter 22

Let's talk about sex

After losing a partner, getting back on the dating scene isn't easy. Not only do you have to face a whole new world of different and new; somewhere along the journey, sex and intimacy come into play.

It's not like it's something you are unfamiliar with, it's just that it's not the same as it was. It will be with someone new. Most of us mature age ladies were brought up by traditional parents, the kind that were just a little past the sexual revolution of the sixties. Sure, they were young, and it was their time, but somehow our parents skipped the sex, drugs and rock and roll and were busy getting married, settling down and having kids of their own and the peace and free love was ahead of our time.

We grew up with our parents' traditional values of love and marriage. Some of us have lived by this code; others have moved forward; adopted the waves of feminism and embraced the freedoms of living in what is always called a man's world. There

Kissing Toads

are others of us who have blended what we call the best of both worlds. After all, it's all about choice.

There is nothing wrong with valuing the tradition of marriage, a commitment to one person, raising a family and growing old together, but what happens when this is no longer possible, when it's been stolen from you and you still want companionship and love and everything you were going to have. It's alright to still want this, and it's okay to go looking for it and start again.

So, you have made the big decision to try dating and for a lot of women; me included, this is a huge step. We crave companionship but we are really anxious about this next step – putting ourselves out there and trying to find that someone we click with.

Experience has taught me you are probably going to meet many people before you meet that someone you really like; that someone who could be identified as a good fit and ticks all the boxes.

Eventually, the question about sex will arise. The question may not be in words but in actions, touches or just the way you are feeling – remember those endorphins I mentioned earlier, the ones like chocolate? Yep, they are taking control of how you feel.

No matter how the message is relayed, remember **the Golden Rule #1**; you make the rules:

- Don't feel pressured. If you are not ready, you are not ready.
- Don't be scared to say how you feel.
- Always use a condom, pregnancy may be off the agenda, but HIV and other sexually transmitted diseases aren't. Don't take risks.

Let's talk about sex

How do you know when it's the right time for sex? There really is no answer to this question, as it's up to you. Remember the **Golden Rule – Rule #1.**

Our generation is the tail-end of the baby boomer generation and is more than likely to take our time and wait a little longer. With our experience and maturity, we realise there are emotional consequences attached to sexual relationships. We also have the desire for sex to be meaningful. We don't want to feel used or use someone – well, most of us don't want to do this.

Casual sex is fine if it's clear that it's what you and your partner both want. We are consenting adults and should not be afraid of making our needs and desires known.

Try to remember, sex is only one component of a relationship, so don't let it become a major factor. If you do, you are bound to become disappointed. Remind yourself of the *'upstairs for thinking'* mantra.

Sex needs to be a topic of discussion if you feel you are heading in that direction. A lot of women of our generation see sex as a commitment. However, it's not always the same story with our male counterparts. We all have physical and emotional boundaries, so make sure you are both clear on the boundaries – this is a must.

Okay, so you think you are ready for sex? Then what do you think about? What are some of the crazy thoughts that go through your head? No matter what, we all have these crazy thoughts it goes with that first time feeling of so long ago.

Let's walk through the crazy thought process step by step – well to a point and remember, anything is possible.

Kissing Toads

1. Getting undressed.

   - How do I take my clothes off while engaged in a passionate kiss without giving him an elbow in the eye?
   - What about that belt buckle that won't undo and looks like it will destroy the moment?

Don't let it worry you, it's all part of the moment; along with the socks that are still on your feet. You will figure it out.

2. The machinery isn't working.

   - What happens when the moment has disappeared? The erection is gone or I'm just not, well ... lubricated?

Hmm, it might have been a little too exciting for him, or maybe a bit more foreplay might help you along the way. Otherwise, there is always Plan B, turn the telly on, have a few snacks along with a cuddle or two and start again.

3. How do I deal with feeling physically uncomfortable?

   - Sometimes amongst all the excitement, a knee or an elbow might cause a little discomfort, not what you want right now. After all, by this stage it is all systems go!

A simple answer here, just tell him to move whatever body part it is as it's in the way and you are not comfortable.

4. Communication

   - Should we engage in flirtatious, exciting or teasing type talk?

Let's talk about sex

- Should we talk about what we like and what we don't?
- How do I know when I should talk and when it's best not to say anything at all?

The answer to all the above is it's up to you! Some people enjoy that thing called teasing; it stimulates the mood. If you don't like it or it's not your thing, please try not to laugh. Nothing will kill the moment more than being laughed at.

Not everyone is good at communication and sometimes partners will try different approaches to see what you like. You are in this moment too, so there is nothing wrong with changing the conversation to something you want to hear; this is where you could talk about what you like and sometimes it's good not to say anything at all and just move your partner's hands to where you want them or try guiding him / her with your eyes and your body language.

5. It's not happening for me.

- The night seemed perfect. You are both in the mood and you feel you should reach that critical point, but an orgasm isn't happening and sadly you know it will not happen even though it's been really great sex. What's happening?

Sometimes, no matter how many skyrockets are in flight, it's just not going to happen. Don't be hard on yourself or your partner; life would have taught you that not everyone reaches a climax every time, even with incredible sex. If you don't believe this, it's time to get the old Sex and the City DVDs out and rewind to some of Samantha and Carrie's misadventures in bed. It happens; accept it. After all, everything else was fantastic, wasn't it?

Just for interest, I searched the web to see if I could find how long women can remain sexually active. As they say 'just asking for a friend' ☺

I found an article by Luke Yoquinto (2013) that said, *'Sex life becomes more satisfying for women after forty'*. It went on to say that the researchers surveyed a group of women between ages 40 and 100, with a median age of 67. Half of the responders said they were sexually active, and most of those women said they could become aroused, maintain lubrication and achieve orgasm during sex, even after the age of 80.

Among sexually active women, those who were below age 55 or above 80 were the most likely to report satisfaction with their ability to achieve orgasms. Wow, how's that for news!

This Live Science article is a few years old, but it's worth a read so I have included the link in the back of this book.

6. That other thing that gets in the way – Menopause.

Sex doesn't end at menopause, no way. Unfortunately for us mature aged ladies, this is something we all have to face, be aware of and know how to work with it. Let's face it, we are all getting older and our bodies are changing and we have to learn to deal with it. If you read my web search above, you will know there is a sex life after menopause, and if you are lucky, you might still enjoy it in your eighties. It's said that the key to great sex after fifty is to know your body and its changes so you can understand what your needs are. Once you understand your body and know your needs, you will know what gives you pleasure.

Let's talk about sex

With menopause comes a natural drop in estrogen, which can leave you very dry. How do I know? —been there (talk to your doctor) Pain and discomfort can become a real issue and if left untreated, it can lead to other problems such as atrophy.

For a lot of women, a good lubricant you can pick up from the chemist or even some supermarkets is all you need, but for others it might be a topical estrogen to help repair the damage being done. Note: add lubricant to the toolbox!

It's important for your partner to understand this too, so he knows how to work with you to ensure you are both enjoying physical intimacy. Also, take note that if he is in the same age bracket, there may be changes he is experiencing as well, so work together and make it enjoyable!

It is important to remember for those of us mature aged daters there is no age limit on having sex. We have got older, our bodies have changed; our lives have changed. Sexual satisfaction depends more on the overall quality of a relationship. It's not about proving anything at our age, we have already done that.

7. Respect

You note that throughout my journey, I haven't shared the sexual side of my encounters; this in part, is out of respect for those men that I have spent time with. Like everyone else, I have had some good sexual encounters and some, well; we just won't talk about them. I have at times also felt used, but I learnt quickly not to let this happen again.

Sometimes there are no dos or don'ts, no right ways or wrong ways. Every situation is unique and feelings are different. Do what's right

Kissing Toads

for you and feel comfortable with your decision. Initiating sex can be just as frightening for some men too. With all the issues behind the *#MeToo* movement and the *It's Not Okay* campaign, some men are unsure how they should approach sex with a new partner.

The media has brought a lot of inappropriate behaviour to the public eye and that's a good thing. We can all learn from it and we should. We should all have enough respect for each other to know when sex is okay and when it's not. No, still means no.

Make sure you include sex in your conversations. Make sure you both know where you stand and respect each other's values and decisions.

Let's talk about sex

Chapter 23

It's definitely not just me

Why is it that some women meet men who can treat them right and other women are so unlucky with relationships? Every toad in the book seems to head toward some of the most beautiful, caring women I know.

Even though my relationships to date haven't had that fairy tale ending, I can at least say each of my dates so far have behaved appropriately. They have been real gentlemen in their behaviour towards me. Some bad manners and a few things to learn, but overall, they have not made me feel scared or in any danger.

> *'It is the law of nature that woman should be held under the dominance of man'*
> **Confucius**

This is the same great philosopher, politician, and teacher who believed that all people and the society they live in benefit from a lifetime of learning and moral outlook. His messages of knowledge,

Kissing Toads

benevolence, loyalty, and virtue were the main guiding philosophy of China for thousands of years. This same benevolent man encouraged social injustice towards women.

Confucianism turned marriage into the bondage of women; treating them as possessions of their husbands. (Gao, Xiongya. 2003)

How would you feel when you think you have met your perfect match and the more you try to make it work, the more you make excuses for his behaviours? You accept things that are not okay - are okay. You pay for everything, love his children and you don't worry about the little things he doesn't do for you. How would you feel? Hurt, used, lonely, exhausted, even worthless? I think the answer is all the above.

It's hard to explain or understand that even when you can see what is happening and attempt to make him feel something for you - it just doesn't work.

Even the most sensible of women can make mistakes. They can see what is happening, but they want to make things work; then after having so much demeaning behaviour inflicted on them, these sensible women are exhausted, totally exhausted, even humiliated, they have had enough and finally give up; and rightly so.

I have used the term give up, however, this should be taken in the positive context as what it actually means is that these women have finally found the strength and empowerment to admit they are better than this and deserve much better and so ends the relationship.

No woman, in fact, no person, deserves to be treated in such a misogynistic way. No woman deserves humiliation, disrespect, belittlement or to be used.

It's definitely not just me

It is horrible what you hear. I have listened to women crying over demeaning treatment when all they have tried to do is feel good about themselves as a person. Where women have spent some time and effort on themselves only to be told things like you look like a slut or what's wrong with you or sometimes they are just totally ignored. Then again, no attention and being ignored is better than being told you look like a slut.

Misogynistic scarring is deep; it's hurtful and very hard to recover from. Confidence and self-worth are destroyed and just when you think you have got through it; something big or even small happens, and it takes you back to that dark place of worthlessness.

Sadly, I have watched this happen, and it's cruel. This is where a good friend needs to be there to remind you that you are a good person, or sometimes they just need to be there to give you a hug and pour you a wine and remind you how brave you were to dump that no good arsehole.

I'm not going to say it's a good friend's job to criticise how you manage the relationship because we are all different and it could destroy a friendship or worse still, take you out of the picture so you won't know what's happening and won't be there when you are needed. Alarm bells ring in different ways, so friends need to be there to keep their eyes and ears open. Sometimes a friend just needs to be there to help you pick up the pieces. Every situation is unique.

I will not pretend it's easy to bounce back from a bad relationship because it's not. Pain and scarring are deep. The journey back to being you is based on small steps, one at a time, and taking time out for you.

Kissing Toads

"In life, we never lose friends; we only learn who the true ones are."
Author unknown

Chapter 24

Down right dirty!

Girlfriends are supposed to be your rock, the people who you share almost everything with; your fears, anxieties, hopes for the future, everything and anything you want. There is an unwritten rule based on love and trust, but what do you do when that trust is broken?

My dear friend met a man she felt was worth exploring the possibilities of a relationship with. He showed an interest in exploring possibilities too. They had several meaningful conversations. They laughed together and before long they were out together, having fun and dancing the night away. The first night out proved to be so much fun that they got busy planning catch-up number two.

Kissing Toads

In between their catch-ups, there was a lot of phone banter. They were really enjoying each other's company. The second date went well. Following this date, they met up with friends. It was sort of planned. He had a single male friend, and she had a single lady friend. To save confusion, I will give them names.

After a great night out, all four hopped into the car together; his friend Tim and her friend Vicki seemed to have hit it off exceptionally well. They were all over each other, a bit like dogs on heat; sorry but I don't know how else to describe it.

My poor friend felt very uncomfortable. She was worried about Vicki's behaviour and where it might lead. They had only met Tim a couple of hours ago, knew nothing about him. Not only this, but how does this behaviour reflect on my friend? Fortunately, she set her own rules and made it very clear that she does not behave this way.

The night, even though it was uncomfortable, finished well. Both women left safely and my friend was possibly a little cross with Vicki.

Things quietened down a little. The new man called a few times. The banter was pleasant. There was an occasion where he had called to invite her out and at first she had declined as she had already planned to have a dinner catch-up with Vicki, who he had met on the previous date – that uncomfortable night. Anyway, to cut a long story short, he extended the invitation to include both women if they wanted to catch-up after their dinner, so she took him up on this.

The night was going well. The two women met up at the agreed rendezvous point, a local pub close to her man's home; he again had Tim with him. Behaviours were a little more respectful. They laughed and danced and had fun.

Down right dirty!

At the end of the night, both women were invited back to the 'potential man's' home. Tim went along too. As already mentioned, behaviours were respectful, and the night was pleasantly moving along. Tim was ready to go and politely made his exit. My friend was also ready to go but, **AND BIG ALARM BELLS**, Vicki wasn't, and she told my friend that she would make her own way home later. After some discussion, my friend reluctantly left by herself.

The next day, she learnt her potential new man no longer had an interest in her. Suddenly her so called good friend Vicki had become the new love interest.

WTF! How does a friend do this? Never mind what it says about him. What does it say about her and her relationship with her girlfriend, the woman she has shared so much with? It's unforgivable, the trust is broken, the friendship destroyed; the damage is irreparable.

Once again, confidence shattered and that feeling of worthlessness returns. Once again, all of those little steps taken to rebuild herself have just collapsed from under her and she is back to square one. What's worse is, this time she has lost someone who was supposed to be a good friend, and this is sad, really, really sad.

Time moves on and after some of the hurt had healed, it was time for my dear friend to have another go at the dating scene. After all, they say that there is someone out there for everyone or as that dating commercial says, *'someone is finding love every so many minutes'*. Believe what you want. Finding genuine love isn't easy, but if you want it, you have to keep looking.

My beautiful friend has met so many dickheads that you would think she has some sort of magnetic field around her and it draws these ugly toads to her. I am not really sure how someone so smart,

Kissing Toads

gorgeous and absolutely lovable can attract the dickheads that she does. I know that once she finds the right man, he will be the luckiest man on the planet. I'm sure he is out there for her, but jeepers he is difficult to find.

There are other stories you hear too, horrible stories, situations no one would ever want to find themselves in. Stories of set-ups; perceptions that 'she is easy', introducing her to mates on a pretend date or convincing her she has something in common with a mate, so maybe he could introduce her to this mate. They might become friends?

Some men need to wake up and learn women are real people too. We deserve respect and if we give you our trust as friends, don't abuse it.

My friend has had some hard knocks but from all the knocks and put downs and falling down and getting up again, she has taught me a lot.

She has taught me –

- Respecting yourself is your first priority.
- No man is worth sacrificing your own values for.
- If he can't support himself and has no plans, he is a loser.

And

- An ex is an ex for a reason.

Kissing Toads

"It's better to be single and fabulous on your own than it is to settle on a relationship that isn't everything you dreamed it would be."
(Anonymous)

Chapter 25

Meet Terry

Having spent some time away with my grandchildren, I was ready to bounce back. It was time to revisit the dating site and see if I had any messages awaiting my attention or maybe there could be some new faces on board.

One thing about dating sites is that there are some faces that seem to be there all the time. I am not sure if they just can't find the right person or if they treat dating like eating chocolates and they want to try all the different types or maybe they just forgot to cancel their subscription – very easy with automatic renewals.

As I am scrolling through, I see I have a few messages from one man who attracts my interest; that's along with one from the past who keeps offering to try his massage techniques on me! Oh no, no, no; definitely not. Anyway, back to the interesting one; he is local;

Kissing Toads

which is good; single; which is a must, has his own business, great he can support himself. Three ticks so worth exploring further. His profile reads well, so yes, I respond.

Our messages via the dating site all seem to go well. After a few nights of messages on the site, he asks for my phone number so we can talk. I agree and it's all very pleasant. We plan to catch-up and we set a date.

As we are talking, we discover we visit a lot of the same places and it just so happened that we were both going to dinner at the same hotel with our groups of friends on the same night. We decided to use this occasion as a chance to say hello.

Thinking back on this, it probably wasn't such a good idea. Don't impose a complete stranger on friends before you have really had the time to meet them yourself!

As I say, I'm learning lessons all the time.

Anyway, back to dinner. We caught sight of each other and met away from our tables. He seemed okay. Our meeting was very brief; after all, we were with our individual groups of friends. At the end of the night, his crowd had gone, and he came to say goodbye to me. I invited him to join us – blame it on the wine!

It was just a drink and a chat – well, a chat with ten other people and me. He then politely left. I went home. Later in the evening, I got a message saying he was looking forward to our catch-up and I must admit, so was I.

Coffee catch-up – well what can I say, usual protocol. Café by the beach, lots of first date conversation. All seemed to go really good.

Meet Terry

Well, it started on a good note and then he started talking about his ex and his daughter, neither of whom speak to him. I felt sorry for him knowing he had no relationship with his only child; I don't know how I would cope without my children in my life.

Like it or not, I brought this conversation to a close; after all, it's a first date, and I truly didn't want to encourage a bitter conversation and this is where it was heading. As you know, I had a happy marriage, so I'm not familiar with all the anger and hate some folks have between them. It couldn't have been all bad; they must have loved each other somewhere along the way.

We have all been hurt one way or another and somehow we all need to deal with it as best we can. We don't all move on, believe me I get it, but you don't impose your ill feelings on others the same way I don't impose my grief. Some things you have to learn to manage internally or let them go.

Our conversation then moved to the dating site, who we had met, what we had read. How we liked or didn't like what we had read. I spoke of my fondness for the two elderly gentlemen that I had met on the site and how they had become like adopted fathers to me. We spoke about loneliness and how difficult it must be for my lovely older guys.

I guess their loneliness was the reason I kept in touch; there was nothing to it, just a friendly hello now and then or an update on what I had been up to, who I had met, that sort of thing.

Sometimes the guys would talk about their wives and the lives they lived, other times they would talk about their travels or the veggie garden, or even about their cars. I didn't mind, it was always pleasant to talk with them. They had adored their wives and you could easily pick up on this by the words they used.

Kissing Toads

Anyway, back to my date. I moved our conversation once again to explore what we had in common and there seemed to be a lot. Music; movies; travel; the list was quite long. Our coffee turned into two, then three coffees and then, all coffeed out; it was time to go. Date number two was agreed for the next weekend.

Once again, there were the in between date phone conversations – all good, just the how was your day sort of talk. Date night arrives, a meal at the local pub, nothing extravagant, just good, lots of conversation and a few laughs. A pleasant night out!

After dinner, it was coffee at my place, just coffee, and we made plans for date number three.

The week seemed to go by quickly, but I didn't hear from him. I knew he had a lot of work on, so I thought I should leave him alone as he is probably tired – here I go making excuses again! Thursday came and went, Friday night nothing; then Saturday morning a message to tell me it was over and not to contact him ever again.

To say I was a little confused is an understatement. I wanted to know what on earth I had done to trigger such a response, so bugger it, like it or not, he was getting a call from me because I am big enough to do things properly!

I could sense the friction when he answered my call, after saying hello and then realising it was me he went very quiet, that sort of angry quiet that you can somehow sense. I asked him not to hang up and could he at least tell me what had happened.

I let him know I was confused, and that it was fine if he didn't want to see me, but what on earth had I done? He bluntly responded with, *"I can see you are still on the dating site, so if you are busy looking*

Meet Terry

to see who else is out there; don't waste my time". I composed myself by counting to three and taking a deep breath. I could have asked him what he was doing on the dating site, but I chose not to as no matter what this relationship was over – my call.

I politely reminded him of the conversation we had on the first date, where I had told him about my two elderly gentlemen and how I keep in touch with them. I had been upfront about this from that first date and there were no other intentions, just a friendly touch base. He knew I was rather fond of them. I then said goodbye and hung up.

Shortly afterwards, I received a text message. He apologised. He asked me if I could forgive him and pretend it never happened. Could we start again? I didn't respond.

About an hour later, another message; this time he told me what I think was the truth. A woman he had been dating before me had sold up and had moved closer to him. She wanted to re-establish her relationship with him. Holding myself together, I wished him well and suggested he should have told me the truth in the first place rather than look for something to blame me for to end what could have been our relationship. I had done nothing wrong.

I accept that sometimes things don't work out how you want them to. I accept feelings change and relationships might or might not be worth pursuing, but I didn't and still don't accept lies or wrongly accusing people or the blame game, for f#@%s sake, just be honest.

Shortly after our exchange of texts, I received a very long text message that went like this -

'Dear Julie, I am so sorry. Can you forgive me? I still want to go out with you tonight. The woman I am with, I don't love her. I feel very

Kissing Toads

sorry for her and she sold up and moved down here to be closer to me, so what am I supposed to do? She isn't independent like you. I know she will be a burden. It won't work. I know we could make a go of it if you agree.'

AGREE! Agree to what. Boy, was I angry. I couldn't believe what he had written. This man was the ultimate TOAD.

I responded.

In my reply, I asked if this was some sort of nasty joke. I asked how stupid he thought I was. I asked if he was going to tell that poor woman he was now back with what he was up to. I asked him not to contact me again and then finished my text with something like I hoped he could be man enough to be honest with her.

Funnily enough, I received a short text back from him which said, and I quote, *'I am an honest man; you can ask any of my friends.'* I didn't respond – jerk. The end!

This man was my introduction to involvement with a Toad. I didn't sense it on the radar, but boy am I glad the relationship didn't go any further. I was shaky after our text conversations, but I didn't cry. I didn't blame myself or look inwards for what I might have done wrong. I was actually quite proud of myself for recognising, accepting and dealing with this toad the way I had.

A good movie and a few wines quickly helped me forget this toad. Well, actually I didn't forget him altogether, as I am thankful I had the opportunity to see how much I had grown and the power I had to protect myself and my emotions – I'm learning.

Chapter 26

Meet James

Throughout this journey, I had involved one of my sisters in any potential dates worth exploring – Friday night wine o'clock became a regular progress report meeting. I would fill her in on any profiles I was looking at, most of the time I would read them to her just to get that sisterly professional opinion which she was more than happy to give and she had to put up with me sending  photos of those I thought were worth pursuing. Sisters can be very blunt, but if you want to hear it how it is, ask your sister.

Here I was scrolling through my messages and again one sparked an interest. He had sent a few messages, so maybe it was worth responding. What have I got to lose?

Kissing Toads

I had been on the dating site for six months or more this time around and it was feeling like an awful long time and, to be honest, I was feeling over it. In the back of my mind, I was questioning if dating sites really work.

Maybe I was asking for too much. I am really too old for this! BUT I had paid money to be here, so like a seasoned bargain hunter, I was going to get my money's worth. I know that sounds awful, but I just wanted maybe one last chance because there might be somebody out there for me.

I contacted my potential new interest. Boxes ticked, sounds lovely, lived miles away, that's a downer, but hey let's give it a go!

I mentioned what should be in the toolbox some time ago. Every toolbox should contain at least one sister, so now it's time to make use of her... again. Timing is everything; thank goodness it's a Friday night and wine o'clock is due to get underway. Wine is poured and we are ready to rock! We have to do this by phone as she lives in hillbilly country, no seriously, we live two driving days apart and she lives on a property in her own little piece of heaven.

As we talk and enjoy our wine, I update her on my dating adventures. Not that there had been many; she thinks I'm picky and judgemental and maybe I am, but I've been loved and spoilt and I won't have anything less so yes she is right I am picky and judgemental and even more so after a few wines.

Anyhow, after the update, I give her a rundown on the new man who has sparked my interest. As a good sister should do, she wanted a photo, and she had to know more about him. My wine bottle was nearly empty and I imagine hers was too, so in finishing

Meet James

our conversation I promised I would keep her updated – which I would do anyway, promised or not.

Back to my potential date.

A message arrived asking if I would like to catch-up the following weekend. He worked in a country pub but had the following Sunday off, so maybe we could do lunch? Sounds good to me!

He was happy to drive up to my area, which was good. Lunch was pleasant, yes, a beachside café, just a different one. Conversation flowed and time disappeared, so we planned to have a second catch-up on his next weekend off. It was all good, but if I think about it, all of my first dates have been good, that is all the first dates I went through with.

Seriously, there are reasons you don't go ahead with first dates and there are trigger points that let you know when the flight fight response needs to come into play. For example, if you show up for that first date and you can't recognise who it is you are supposed to be meeting. Maybe his profile picture is not him. If the place he is meeting you doesn't feel safe or even something as simple as your gut instinct tells you something isn't right. Listen to your instinct. If it doesn't feel right then it's not, so high tail out of the place.

As nice as this man was, I was thinking distance and rostered weekends might just impede a relationship – I've been down this path before, but with no commitments at the moment, I am really free to see where this goes and so is he.

My thinking has changed. Six months ago, I would have only focussed on the one person at one time. I would want to see what the possibilities were with the individual, where it was going,

Kissing Toads

and would a relationship develop. I am now learning that all this time I have been trying to be fair to other people and also to my own values, but this hasn't worked so well to date. I still hold my values, but somewhere I also have to look at me and what I want and remind myself to remove the barriers that are preventing me from finding an ideal partner.

This adventure is about me and finding the right person. It could be this man; who knows? I made a decision that even though this man seems very nice, there are a few hurdles in the way and there is no commitment to anything; it's okay to keep my options open. If I want to keep visiting the dating site, I can. Who knows, there could still be someone out there who ticks all the boxes and who will sweep me off my feet!

So here I have to concede, maybe I should have taken the dating site advice and just, in my words, 'shopped around' and had fun meeting new people rather than expecting every encounter to be meaningful.

Over the next week, we messaged a few times. Date number two was cancelled due to work commitments, so we made plans for another catch-up.

Cancelling our date was fine as it helped me rethink long distance relationships, well it's not really too long but over two hours away is a long distance when you are trying to get to know someone and you both have work commitments.

I know many long distance relationships work very well, but we are not yet in a relationship, so the getting to know you part might not work out so well. Remember, I have been there before and while it was fine for over two years, we both came to realise it wasn't

Meet James

going to work. It is hard to get to know a person who you can only see on weekends and even harder when he only wants to see you every second weekend as he has things to do, so yes, I am now cautious with distance.

Friday night has come around again and almost wine o'clock time. Time to report in; wine poured and now it's update time. It's good to have a sounding board of a sister; she will listen to the good, the stupid and the bad in an almost non-judgemental way and then bring you down to earth with a bang. Here I could say how great date one was, what a really nice guy he is and then the pitfalls of trying to make this work – distance and weekend rosters.

While my dear sister was busy putting ordinary life into perspective for me and trying to provide a reality check, I had a hand on my computer mouse, just taking a quick scroll through the dating site. I listened to my sister's wise words and yes, she was right, but in this case I had already decided that I didn't want to commit myself to pursuing the relationship any further.

Kissing Toads

"Self-care is not self-indulgence,
it is self-preservation."
Audre Lorde

Chapter 27

Me time, you time, we all need our time

Here I go again, time for some me time. Time out with friends; time with one particular friend. Yes, the BFF who knows exactly what we – me and her are going through. We were probably pretty awful as we went through our toad hating encounters! Talk about judgemental; but we needed a laugh and a cry and a laugh again.

We honed in on her latest ventures of not what was expected and it was hard not to laugh when she told me about one man on the dance floor who was so busy looking for flaws with her and all he could come up with was a very slight gap in her teeth. I had to ask for a magnifying glass to see if I could find it. How odd – not sure where he escaped from.

Kissing Toads

We shared dating site messages, egged each other on with who we thought we should respond to – it was needed, just a chance to unwind and accept there are crazy people out there.

We made a few MAFS watching dates – for those who aren't accustomed to this acronym; Married at First Sight, and a big thank you to Channel Nine for creating what became our catch-up TV show, which over a few wines became a real laugh for us both – honestly the fun we had with it and the discussion it created, I could write a book on it. ☺

After a few weeks of rebuilding or maybe just a rest, I was ready to try again. After all, there are some good men out there, I am sure of it. I was comfortable using the dating site as I felt safe and I knew that the company had strict guidelines and monitored what was posted and they had acted on profiles I had reported in the past. It sounds weird, women in their fifties, sixties or even older using online dating sites, but it's how things are. Welcome to the world of the web!

This time around I needed very little time to heal or deal with what might have been, or even reassess what I might have done. This chic was getting tough! I wanted to go back online and explore other potential 'winks' or hello messages that were sitting in my dating site mailbox.

Me time, you time, we all need our time

Kissing Toads

"We are all a little weird and life's a little weird, and when we find someone whose weirdness is compatible with ours, we join up with them and fall in mutual weirdness and call it love."
Dr Seuss

Chapter 28

Yes! There is a happy ever after

Back to wine o'clock mode, my Friday night sister time catch-up. I noted that there were several messages on my profile page, honestly it must seem sad that so many of us spend our Friday nights on dating sites. I guess I was lucky that at least I was doing this over a glass of wine with my sister and not on my own.

I had some lovely messages which I shared with her and then others where all we could do was laugh. I guess it's not really funny. We are all trying to find love, but please don't use corny movie quotes when trying to impress. Should that be a rule? No, it's just basic common sense.

Kissing Toads

While receiving loving sisterly advice, I came across a profile that caught my attention. I was immediately attracted to his picture, looked on the taller side, piercing eyes, thick silver hair and a beautiful smile. There was just something about his picture that took me in. My first reaction was, oh my god, is he real? And then I read his profile. Well, this man has tickets on himself! Does he want to employ someone or date them? Honestly, it was like reading a job spec.

I stopped my sister in the middle of delivering her wisdom because I wanted to read her the job specifications I had just read. I think my conversation went something like, *'oh my god, listen to this,'* I then read what was written. Thank goodness it didn't start off with something like *'help wanted'* but *'I am looking for....'* Who does this cocky bastard think he is? He sounds so arrogant! I then decided I was going to show an interest and if he responded, I would love to actually meet him so I could tell him how arrogant he is. Our wine o'clock therapy session finished and, as promised, updates would be provided.

I can't reiterate enough how good it is to have great sisters and great friends. Great children too! But believe me, children don't want to know about their mother's love life. They love you with all their heart and they want you to be happy and, more importantly they want to know you are safe. Well, mine do!

Not only did I continue my wine o'clock, but I also kept up my visits and conversations with friends who understand the dating sites as much as me or even better. So in between watching Married at First Sight, or The Batchelor in Paradise or whatever other finding love reality show we had to critique, we also shared dating advice and misadventures.

Yes! There is a happy ever after

I think we were becoming experts in identifying toads from frogs and over drinks and toad talk one night, I committed to a book about toads and frogs and some rules to help those of us who feel like dinosaurs when it comes to dating. I wanted to put all the lessons learnt so far into a book that might hopefully help other women just like us. Brave women ready to conquer the unknown world of cyber dating!

Now, back to my cocky, arrogant possible date! Yes, I sent a message and yes, I got a response. I was polite, and his response was polite – it wasn't supposed to be, remember I had said he was cocky and arrogant. Cocky and arrogant people aren't polite.

We exchanged quite a few messages through the dating site. I thought this must be a different man. This man seems nice. What I am reading is respectful and ... well, just nice, the sort of nice I would expect, but not from him. What's going on here? I really do like the sound of him. And those eyes! I think this is the first time I have been so taken with features, I mean eyes!

It was a little different this time; he invited me for coffee at a place not far from home. Normally it would be me determining the meeting place, however, I knew this café, and it was actually nice to have someone suggest the meeting place and check to see if I was comfortable in going there.

Our catch-up was a Thursday night rendezvous, which meant it would not be a late night as we both had work the next day. I had already determined it wouldn't be a late night anyway as remember this was that cocky, arrogant man I was determined to tell where to go.

As our catch-up was to be fairly close to home and it was a nice evening, I walked to the café. I had already taken all the necessary

Kissing Toads

precautions for first dates, checked in with the family so they knew where I would be, and planned to call a friend when I got home so they knew I got home. I didn't have to worry about the café as I knew it and my walk home was along a busy beach front so lots of people around – safety wise, all was good and so far no instincts of anything that could go wrong. Safety boxes are ticked and time to go!

I arrived at the chosen destination a little early, only to discover it was closed. Apparently, this was a very new change to the norm, so I had to give my date the benefit of the doubt. This wasn't his fault. Sometimes things just happen.

Plan B, there was a café next door, so I could check this out and make arrangements for us to catch-up here. It was a lovely little café with outside dining, so I knew I could place myself somewhere where I would see him arrive.

He arrived on time, very easy to recognise as he looked just like his profile photo - which was a good start. He was very apologetic and extremely embarrassed about his original plans, but it didn't really matter as we had a lovely table next door and we were overlooking the beach, which was always nice.

This date was different; it was nothing like what I had experienced with all of my first dates until now. I sensed a warmness that wasn't supposed to be there. This is not what I had imagined and the dislike I was sure I would be feeling just wasn't here. It is very hard to build a dislike when you sense the opposite; warm, polite, kind and this is all in the first five minutes. I hate to admit it, but maybe I was wrong. Maybe this time I had been too judgemental.

My date, well dressed, smelt delicious – if I can say that! He appeared to be quite the gentleman and as he spoke, I sensed

Yes! There is a happy ever after

old school values; I really liked this, I liked him! What happened to that cocky, arrogant prick I was going to meet? It's definitely not this man.

Honestly, first date and nearly all the boxes ticked; including boxes I hadn't as yet even thought about. We moved from coffee to a glass of wine and then on to dinner, and the lovely café owners kept the place open just for us. The night, I must say, was THE perfect date.

No! This was all wrong. He wasn't supposed to be nice; he wasn't supposed to show an interest in me. How could he be taking in every word I spoke? I was very confused. I came here tonight thinking I would give him a piece of my mind, but this man had my head spinning. How did I get it so wrong? This is so right.

The night was perfect. It was how it should be, but it had to end. We both agreed that we would like to do it again but made no commitment. He offered to drive me home, but I wanted to walk. I needed to clear my head and do some of that psycho analysing stuff. I am normally a pretty good judge of people, so what happened here?

My conclusion: I think I fell into the trap that dating experts talk about in glossy magazines or these days more so on blog pages. I was looking for all the things I wouldn't like about a person rather than what I actually might like, so in my mind I had conjured up what I expected this man to be before I had even given him a chance to show me the real him.

Maybe his profile reflected his business persona. Maybe I read him too harshly. After all, I was reading his profile flippantly over a wine conversation while scrolling through a mixture of corny and not so interesting messages on my dating site.

Kissing Toads

The other message to myself I noted was that this man was just a little older than what I had said I was looking for. I was looking for someone the same age as me, so widening my search parameters to include an extra five years was probably something I should have thought about earlier.

Lesson learnt – don't be too restrictive. Make sure you give a lot of thought to what you are looking for and then look at where you can expand your options and still achieve your goal. As long as your foundation is strong and you know the basics, remember this is about you. Let yourself build on all the ideals you value.

The walk home helped clear my head; I think it took me longer than normal as I was, as they say, floating on cloud nine. I had never, ever had such a wonderful first date. Then, to my surprise, I found a lovely message on the dating site from this man thanking me for such a wonderful night and he would like to spend some time getting to know me better, if that was okay with me?.

Once I got over my how could I be so wrong about this man and accepting that this could be so right, I was more than happy to respond with a *'would love to catch-up again soon'* message. I mentioned I would be away for the weekend as I was taking the grandchildren on a short holiday, but any other time would be fine.

With a prompt reply acknowledging the importance of grandchildren and a little bit about his grandchildren, which he was very happy to share, we made a date for lunch on the Monday I returned and we exchanged phone numbers.

After making the mandatory I am home now calls so that everyone could be assured I was safe. It was time to accept I was wrong.

Yes! There is a happy ever after

Yes, me! I was very wrong; I think I have met a beautiful man! So far so good, but remember, it's still only a first date perspective.

What this date taught me was that my checklist tick boxes were expanding. From this one date, I was discovering all of these other things that were important to me. They have probably always been there, but just needed a bit of a nudge to bring them to the surface.

On this date I met someone who:

- ✓ Shares my values
- ✓ Appreciates that family is important
- ✓ Can accept that I am a widow who had a wonderful marriage
- ✓ Shares my passion for travel
- ✓ Can accept that there are some sports I'm not really into
- ✓ Was willing to compromise to find things we could enjoy together
- ✓ Could hold an intelligent conversation
- ✓ Wanted to know me better
- ✓ Is well adjusted and ready to rebuild his life
- ✓ Seems to have time for me and my sometimes eccentric ways
- ✓ Makes me laugh
- ✓ I think will love me
- ✓ Makes me feel safe and wanted

At this stage it really is hard to say if the boxes were big ticks, as I kept telling myself to come down to earth, it's very early days and so far only one date but for some funny reason, from the one date and many text messages I felt I could tick all the boxes. It was a case of when you know you know!

Kissing Toads

But how do you know you know? Love has been around for a long time. There isn't a medical description of what to look for. How do you describe feelings when everyone's feelings are different?

As you get older, you also have a different perspective on what love is. What real love is and when you have experienced real love, you don't forget it. It's not all about his kiss, a wedding dress, and a white picket fence. It might have been at twenty, but at fifty you have been there and experienced that phase of love at least once, maybe even twice, but you have been there. As you get older, you value different things.

You want someone to enjoy life with, to share those experiences you had to delay while you were busy raising a family. You want someone to hold hands with while enjoying a sunset or get soaked with while laughing in the rain. It's the little things that mean a lot. Someone who is interested in sharing your day and doesn't mind a few wrinkles or the greying hair and someone who makes you smile and with a big hug makes you feel safe. I was ready to see if this is where this relationship might take me.

Date two came around and, as expected, he ticked all the boxes. We talked, and we talked and we laughed and shared stories. Different people from what seemed like different worlds, but we shared a genuine interest in each other and he made it very clear that he really wanted to learn more about me. I'm glad we had the day off, as it was a very long lunch.

Dates three, then four, then five; it just kept going, each one better than the last, if that's possible. The how do you know he is the right one or how do you know you are falling in love? Well, these answers were coming to me. You still question them as I remember falling in love once before, but this time it felt different; it wasn't hard. I

Yes! There is a happy ever after

didn't have to make excuses for anything. This man was happy to meet my friends and do things I liked to do. We just clicked.

I was actually happier than I had been in a very long time. I was developing strong and genuine feelings for this man, even though I hadn't known him for very long. I felt a love and respect that I didn't think existed anymore. I learnt those butterflies in the stomach actually exist when it's real.

How do you know you are in love?

- ♥ You become a genuinely happier person
- ♥ You miss him when he isn't around, even though you only saw him hours ago
- ♥ The butterflies – they just won't settle
- ♥ You feel nervous, excited and anxious all at the same time
- ♥ Everything feels new and worthwhile
- ♥ Everything feels easy
- ♥ You feel comfortable and safe
- ♥ And you just want to be in his arms

Falling in love when you are older is more about substance. We get to a point where we can see past physical beauty; even if he has the most gorgeous eyes and a brilliant smile, his words and actions mean so much more.

Most of us have lived full and interesting lives. We have achieved the goals and expectations we set as a young married couple. The kids have grown up, and we are approaching retirement, if not already retired.

It's a whole new world out there when you suddenly find that the person who you made life long plans with is no longer there to

Kissing Toads

see the plan through, but even with the curved ball thrown your way, sometimes you have to catch it, hold it and then throw it in a new direction.

I wanted to find a person of substance, someone who had goals and ambitions; not the sort of ambitions a successful career brings, but goals and ambitions that come with being older, those we dreamt about doing once the kids were off our hands and time belonged to us. As you grow older, you ask yourself more relevant questions about falling in love before you move into a new relationship.

As we get older, we are more serious about life. We are clear on what we want. Love becomes more about depth, what truly matters. It may mean companionship, warmth, affection. We don't tolerate games, bad behaviour, cheating or lies – no red flags or alarms.

So how do you know when you are in love? You just know!

How do you know if it will last? You don't!

Our journeys are all different; we learn so many new things along the way so don't be afraid to try something new. We meet all kinds of people throughout our individual journeys, and each person is there for a reason. Some stay and some leave; be it a short time or a longer time. It's still your journey and every person who joins you along the way leaves you with something; a memory, a lesson, a friendship or a gift; be that love, encouragement or empowerment, there are so many gifts we collect along the way and each deserves to be acknowledged.

My journey is continuing; one thousand four hundred and sixty days later, I am still enjoying every new day. I think I have found my happy ever after. I would like to believe I am creating my own

Yes! There is a happy ever after

real life fairy tale. After all, I have kissed my frog many times, and he has shown me that he really is a very charming prince.

This brings me to my last rule: **Rule #10**

Be gracious and accept everyone and everything you gain on your journey; it's all part of life's lessons and it all makes you, you.

'Never lose hope, and if you can, find the courage to love again'
Danielle Steel

The toad refresher!
(And where to learn more)

Golden rules

Rule 1: You make the rules.
Rule 2: You have a right to change the rules.
Rule 3: If rule 1 fails, go back to rule 2.

The rules - <u>Dating sites</u>

1. Check the sites out.
2. Look at joining terms and conditions.
3. Check what you are paying for and the length of the contract.
4. Does the site talk about your safety as a user?
5. How easy is the site to use?
6. Am I comfortable using it?

Kissing Toads

The rules – <u>looking after you</u>

7. Be aware.
8. Maintain your standards and don't settle for less.
9. Your safety is paramount.
10. Be gracious, and accept everyone and everything you gain on your journey.

Most important rule: Use your common sense

Important things to remember

- Trust your instinct.
- Stick to your rules.
- Keep family and friends in your life.
- Have a toolbox ready to use.
- Honesty is everything.
- Be kind to yourself.
- Report all toads.
- Respect yourself – a priority.
- No man is worth sacrificing your values for.
- Never make excuses for bad behaviour.
- If he can't support himself and has no plans, he is a loser.
- Always have a Plan B.
- This is about you.
- An ex is an ex for a reason.
- If it doesn't feel right, it's not right.

Modern dating etiquette

You can contact a potential dating candidate if –

- Your gut instinct tells you it's okay.
- You see some potential worth exploring.
- You maintain your standards.
- You keep your safety as your number one priority.

Respond to messages politely -

- If someone goes to the trouble of sending a message to you, it is always polite to respond. They have gone to the trouble of writing to you, so even if it's only a no thank you; make sure it's polite. It says a lot about your character.

Kissing Toads

- If you receive a wink or other emoticon – then it's up to you, not much effort goes into this sort of response. Just remember it could be a shy person or first time dater, so check the profile first.
- Corny messages you will find are generally system generated, so don't feel obliged to respond.
- Remember, there are a lot of lonely people out there and some just want to chat. You decide if you want to respond, but make sure the rules are clear. If it's just a chat, make it clear it's just a chat or where your interests lie.

What date should you kiss?

- Completely up to you. Kissing sends many different messages, so be clear about why you are doing it. A peck on the cheek says thank you. Something more passionate could imply the wrong message, be clear as to what you want. Don't put pressure on yourself if you aren't ready to lock lips or it just doesn't feel right don't do it.

How many dates before you sleep together?

- How long is a piece of string? There is no set rule on when you initiate sleeping together, the same as there is no set rule on kissing or holding hands. It has to be when you are ready. Remember the Golden Rule – look at rule number 1.

Don't set yourself up to fail

- Go on your date with a positive attitude. If you go out there looking for fault in your date, that is all you will see. Look at what attracted you to this person in the first place.

The first date

Who should initiate the first date?

In this day and age, does it matter? Just make sure it is somewhere you are comfortable with. I can't reiterate enough, safety is paramount.

Who should pay?

More often than not, a gentleman will normally foot the bill; however, there are no strict rules, no obligations. Sometimes it's best to pay for your own coffee or even split the bill.

What should you NOT do on your first date?

- Don't get too excited – it's early days.

Kissing Toads

- Don't talk about your finances.
- Don't give out your address or phone number until you are comfortable to do so.
- Don't be afraid to leave if you don't feel safe. Trust your instinct.
- Don't talk about your ex.
- Don't play on your phone.
- Don't get distracted.
- Never make excuses for bad behaviour.

What you should do on your first date

- Show up on time or call if you are running late.
- Dress to impress or at least make an effort, presentation means a lot.
- Make sure you have advised friends/family of your date, where you are and when you should be getting home.
- Feel free to leave if you feel unsafe.
- Be attentive – focus on your date and the conversation.
- Be polite, manners are a must even in this day and age.
- Look for what you like about your date.
- Offer to split the bill.
- Don't drink too much.
- If you have enjoyed the night, follow up with a thankyou message.
- If it's not going to work, say so.

Red flag alerts – <u>and this is just some of them</u>

	Red flag alert	What to do
1	Shifts the blame for his own actions	'No responsibility for his actions - get rid of him
2	If you don't do….then I'm breaking up with you	Time for him to go
3	I'm brutally honest	Yes, brutal – time to go
4	All my exes are crazy	End it before it starts
5	I don't get angry easily, but when I do	Run before you get hurt
6	Telling you to 'Get over it'	Time to tell him to leave
7	My way or the highway	It's time for the highway
8	I trust you, but I don't trust…..	Trust issues – deal breaker, he goes
9	You're pathetic	Definitely time to go
10	You're so needy	You don't need him

Kissing Toads

	Red flag alert	What to do
11	It was a mistake, I won't do it again	1. Was it? – maybe something minor, so perhaps a second chance 2. Not so minor - Yes, he will. Don't make the mistake of forgiving
12	I don't want to see/meet your friends	You don't want to be isolated – get rid of him
13	It's all about him	No! You are supposed to be his priority
14	He has you second guessing	It's undermining – games aren't cool. Get out
15	He doesn't listen or want to listen to you	What you say isn't important, so neither is he
16	He mocks my goal, my hopes and my dreams	He's insecure, not on the same page. Leave!
17	He doesn't recognise your efforts	Does he really care? – you don't need him
18	You've never met his friends or family	Why? what is he hiding?
19	He doesn't look like his profile picture at all	High tail it out of there
20	He doesn't do what he says he will	Unreliable, a liar. What is he playing at? Go!
21	He doesn't talk about the future	There isn't one, so don't waste your time

Red flag alerts –and this is just some of them

	Red flag alert	What to do
22	He is very secretive	What is he hiding? Beware of the wolf!
23	He stands you up often	There are plenty more fish in the sea! End it
24	He is pressuring you for sex.	No respect – Stick to your values, No means no
25	He makes you feel bad about yourself.	You are better than that. Get rid of the asshole!

The tool box items

Every tool box needs to include

- Sisters.
- Good friends.
- Some me time.
- Some wine – already chilled and ready to drink.
- A cone of silence.
- A dose of reality television.
- At least five chick flicks.
- Movie nights.
- Dinners.
- A pair of big girl pants.
- Lubricant.
- Condoms.
- A good book.
- A comfy bed – this may not fit but a very useful tool.
- Some great 70s or 80s music.

The tick box checklist

This has to be tailored to suit. Only you know what you really want, so make sure you work on this as a priority.

Here's mine

- ✓ Shares my values
- ✓ Appreciates that family is important
- ✓ Can accept that I am a widow who had a wonderful marriage
- ✓ Shares my passion for travel
- ✓ Can accept that there are some things I'm not really into
- ✓ Is willing to compromise
- ✓ Can hold an intelligent conversation
- ✓ Wants to know me better
- ✓ Is well adjusted and ready to build a life with me
- ✓ Has time for me and my sometimes eccentric ways
- ✓ Makes me laugh
- ✓ Will love me
- ✓ Makes me feel safe and wanted
- ✓ Respects me
- ✓ Wants to grow old with me

The dating dictionary

Things have certainly changed in the world of words, particularly dating text. It's like a whole new language. To save you the trouble of having to decipher all the newer vocabulary, I am sharing everything I have already checked out on Google.

Let's start with those acronyms that seem to be so popular in the dating world:

BBW	Big, beautiful woman	BF	boyfriend
D	divorced	HWP	height weight proportion
GF	girlfriend	LD	light drinker
LS	light smoker	SD	social drinker
TS	transsexual	TV	transvestite
GBLTQ	gay, lesbian bi sexual transgender queer	BHM	Big handsome man
MWC	Married with children	TDH	Tall, dark and handsome

Kissing Toads

420	Friendly user of cannabis or tolerant of user	NBM	Never been married
BRB	Be right back	DTE	Down to earth
F2F	Face to face	FOMO	Fear of missing out
FTTB	For the time being	FWB	Friend with benefits
GSOH	Good sense of humour	IRL	In real life
FTA	Fun travel adventure	MBA	Married but available
ISO	In search of	LDR	Long distance relationship
LTR	Long term relationship	MOTOS	Members of the opposite sex
MOTSS	Members of the same sex	PDA	Public display of affection
ROFL	Rolling on the floor laughing	SO	Significant other
TLC	Tender loving care	WAA	will answer all

Breadcrumbing	Sending flirty messages to keep a potential lover interested
Catfish	Someone who creates a false identity online
Ghost	Someone who drops contact without explanation
Haunting	When an ex-partner appears in your life
Jelly	Jealous
Kitten Fishing	Not being honest on your dating profile, stretching the truth
Kray Bae	Crazy baby

The dating dictionary

Layby	Someone you are dating while waiting for better options
Love bombing	A deceptive action, new partner goes over the top with gifts, gestures, and attention.
Monkey	Someone who moves quickly from one relationship to the next
Netflix and Chill	In dating terms it is usually an invitation for having sex
Orbiting	No longer interested but continues to follow you on social media.
Peacocking	Dressing up for social media
R-Bombed	When your love interest ignores your messages
Situationship	Relationship isn't clear defined by either party
Slay	Gets lots of dates
Textlationship	A relationship based only on digital contact
Thirst trap	A picture posted only to attract attention
Thirsty	Desperate for a relationship
Uncuffing	Ditching a long term partner
Unicorn	An individual willing to join an existing relationship, or rare and desirable
X-Factor	A very special personal quality
YODO	You only dump once
Zombie	A ghost who reappears in your life

Reference links for information you might want to read

https://www.eastoftheweb.com/short-stories/UBooks/FrogPrin.shtml. The Frog Prince

https://ideas.ted.com/tag/marilyn-yalom/ - The amorous heart: An unconventional history of love

https://www.urbandictionary.com/define.php?term=Toad the definition of a toad

https://www.scamwatch.gov.au/types-of-scams/dating-romance. Reporting scammers

Military Romance Scams – All About Scammers Posing as Soldiers - Payback. https://payback-ltd.com/blogs/military-romance-scams-all-about-scammers-posing-as-soldiers/

https://books.google.com.au/books/about/The_Penguin_Book_of_Etiquette.html?id=yq9XdGoHHWQC&redir_esc=y The Australian Guide to Modern Manners

https://www.elitedaily.com/p/heres-why-dating-today. Why we make dating so hard

Kissing Toads

https://www.cosmopolitan.com/sex-love/a8259903/second-date-more-important-than-the-first/

Helen Reddy - I Am Woman (1971) - YouTube

https://www.nma.gov.au/defining-moments/resources/first-women-in-parliament

Luke Yoquinto (May 2013) - https://www.livescience.com/36073-women-sex-life-age.html

Gao, Xiongya.(2003)"Women Existing for Men: Confucianism and Social Injustice against Women in China." Race, Gender & Class, vol. 10, no. 3, 2003, pp. 114–125. JSTOR, https://www.jstor.org/stable/41675091?seq=1 :

https://www.esafety.gov.au/women/being-social/online-dating (a worthwhile site to visit)

https://www.purelovequotes.com/author/anonymous/its-okay-to-be-scared-but-you-have-to-get/

https://wordstemple.com/awesome-love-quotes

https://www.livescience.com/36073-women-sex-life-age.html

https://quotessayings.net/topics/better-be-single/

Cyber definitions:

https://www.cyberdefinitions.com/digital_dating_abbreviations_acronyms_slang.html

https://gatekeeperpress.com/book-disclaimer/

About the Author

Julie moved to South Australia 44 years ago with her husband. They married in Whyalla, then moved to Adelaide where they made their home, raised two boys and a menagerie of pets, dogs, cats, kangaroos and possums.

Julie started her career as a veterinary nurse and then completed post graduate studies in business management while working in various public service roles.

Over the years, she has been active in her community at both a Local and State level, represented South Australia in trade delegations, and has taken a strong stand on human rights, animal rights and vilification issues.

Life changed drastically for Julie when her husband was diagnosed with a terminal cancer. Julie's story is about life following loss and grief and all the trials and tribulations of being on your own again and trying for a second chance. Julie takes you on her bumpy journey through the online dating world. It's a story she wants to share in the hope that it gives other women the confidence to have a second chance at a relationship after losing that special someone who rocked their world.

Acknowledgements

Who would have thought a book on dating for women over 50 was ever needed? Certainly not me or hundreds of others who are looking for that someone to share their life with when their world goes to pieces and you are left to start again.

Talking about and even attempting relationships the second time around wasn't easy, but it was made easier with all of the love, support and encouragement I have had along the way.

To my friend June thank you for giving me the courage and showing me how to use online dating sites, my friend Michelle who after a few wines and critiques over reality TV dating shows encouraged me to write about our adventures in the world of online dating.

To my sisters for being there whenever needed, Sue at wine o'clock on Friday nights where she would debrief with me over dating site responses and try to reel in my, at times somewhat judgemental attitude and Sharon for keeping my ideas in perspective. My Chardy sisters who are always there to keep the sun shining, and two very special people who supported me through some very rocky times (thanks Joan and Lawrie).

Kissing Toads

To the men I have met along the way, some who taught me it is possible to have a second chance, some who taught me lessons and empowered me, and one in particular who has given me my happily ever after.

To the Ultimate 48 Hour Author team, thank you for your guidance and for believing in me through my writing and publishing journey.

Most importantly, to my boys Daniel and Ryan, who have been to hell and back with me, shared the pain and helped rebuild our lives – you guys are my everything.

Things for me to note

Kissing Toads

Things for me to note

www.ingramcontent.com/pod-product-compliance
Lightning Source LLC
Chambersburg PA
CBHW030037100526
44590CB00011B/238